Business Model Innovation
Complete Self-Assessment Guide

The guidance in this Self-Assessment is based c
Innovation best practices and standards in business process architecture,
design and quality management. The guidance is also based on the
professional judgment of the individual collaborators listed in the
Acknowledgments.

Table of Contents

About The Art of Service

The Art of Service, Business Process Architects since 2000, is dedicated to helping stakeholders achieve excellence.

Defining, designing, creating, and implementing a process to solve a stakeholders challenge or meet an objective is the most valuable role… In EVERY group, company, organization and department.

Unless you're talking a one-time, single-use project, there should be a process. Whether that process is managed and implemented by humans, AI, or a combination of the two, it needs to be designed by someone with a complex enough perspective to ask the right questions.

Someone capable of asking the right questions and step back and say, 'What are we really trying to accomplish here? And is there a different way to look at it?'

With The Art of Service's Standard Requirements Self-Assessments, we empower people who can do just that — whether their title is marketer, entrepreneur, manager, salesperson, consultant, Business Process Manager, executive assistant, IT Manager, CIO etc... —they are the people who rule the future. They are people who watch the process as it happens, and ask the right questions to make the process work better.

Contact us when you need any support with this Self-Assessment and any help with templates, blue-prints and examples of standard documents you might need:

http://theartofservice.com
service@theartofservice.com

Acknowledgments

This checklist was developed under the auspices of The Art of Service, chaired by Gerardus Blokdyk.

Representatives from several client companies participated in the preparation of this Self-Assessment.

In addition, we are thankful for the design and printing services provided.

Included Resources - how to access

Included with your purchase of the book is the Business Model Innovation Self-Assessment Spreadsheet Dashboard which contains all questions and Self-Assessment areas and auto-generates insights, graphs, and project RACI planning - all with examples to get you started right away.

How? Simply send an email to
access@theartofservice.com
with this books' title in the subject to get the Business Model Innovation Self Assessment Tool right away.

You will receive the following contents with New and Updated specific criteria:

- The latest quick edition of the book in PDF

- The latest complete edition of the book in PDF, which criteria correspond to the criteria in...

- The Self-Assessment Excel Dashboard, and...

- Example pre-filled Self-Assessment Excel Dashboard to get familiar with results generation

- In-depth specific Checklists covering the topic

- Project management checklists and templates to assist with implementation

INCLUDES LIFETIME SELF ASSESSMENT UPDATES

Every self assessment comes with Lifetime Updates and Lifetime Free Updated Books. Lifetime Updates is an industry-first feature which allows you to receive verified self assessment updates, ensuring you always have the most accurate information at your fingertips.

Get it now- you will be glad you did - do it now, before you forget.

Send an email to **access@theartofservice.com** with this books' title in the subject to get the Business Model Innovation Self Assessment Tool right away.

Your feedback is invaluable to us

If you recently bought this book, we would love to hear from you! You can do this by writing a review on amazon (or the online store where you purchased this book) about your last purchase! As part of our continual service improvement process, we love to hear real client experiences and feedback.

How does it work?
To post a review on Amazon, just log in to your account and click on the Create Your Own Review button (under Customer Reviews) of the relevant product page. You can find examples of product reviews in Amazon. If you purchased from another online store, simply follow their procedures.

What happens when I submit my review?
Once you have submitted your review, send us an email at review@theartofservice.com with the link to your review so we can properly thank you for your feedback.

Purpose of this Self-Assessment

This Self-Assessment has been developed to improve understanding of the requirements and elements of Business Model Innovation, based on best practices and standards in business process architecture, design and quality management.

It is designed to allow for a rapid Self-Assessment to determine how closely existing management practices and procedures correspond to the elements of the Self-Assessment.

The criteria of requirements and elements of Business Model Innovation have been rephrased in the format of a Self-Assessment questionnaire, with a seven-criterion scoring system, as explained in this document.

In this format, even with limited background knowledge of

Business Model Innovation, a manager can quickly review existing operations to determine how they measure up to the standards. This in turn can serve as the starting point of a 'gap analysis' to identify management tools or system elements that might usefully be implemented in the organization to help improve overall performance.

How to use the Self-Assessment

On the following pages are a series of questions to identify to what extent your Business Model Innovation initiative is complete in comparison to the requirements set in standards.

To facilitate answering the questions, there is a space in front of each question to enter a score on a scale of '1' to '5'.

1 Strongly Disagree

2 Disagree

3 Neutral

4 Agree

5 Strongly Agree

Read the question and rate it with the following in front of mind:

'In my belief,
the answer to this question is clearly defined'.

There are two ways in which you can choose to interpret this statement;
1. how aware are you that the answer to the question is clearly defined
2. for more in-depth analysis you can choose to gather

evidence and confirm the answer to the question. This obviously will take more time, most Self-Assessment users opt for the first way to interpret the question and dig deeper later on based on the outcome of the overall Self-Assessment.

A score of '1' would mean that the answer is not clear at all, where a '5' would mean the answer is crystal clear and defined. Leave emtpy when the question is not applicable or you don't want to answer it, you can skip it without affecting your score. Write your score in the space provided.

After you have responded to all the appropriate statements in each section, compute your average score for that section, using the formula provided, and round to the nearest tenth. Then transfer to the corresponding spoke in the Business Model Innovation Scorecard on the second next page of the Self-Assessment.

Your completed Business Model Innovation Scorecard will give you a clear presentation of which Business Model Innovation areas need attention.

Business Model Innovation Scorecard Example

Example of how the finalized Scorecard can look like:

Business Model Innovation Scorecard

Your Scores:

BEGINNING OF THE SELF-ASSESSMENT:

CRITERION #1: RECOGNIZE

INTENT: Be aware of the need for change. Recognize that there is an unfavorable variation, problem or symptom.

In my belief, the answer to this question is clearly defined:

5 Strongly Agree

4 Agree

3 Neutral

2 Disagree

1 Strongly Disagree

1. Why is this needed?
<--- Score

2. Who defines the rules in relation to any given issue?
<--- Score

3. Are you dealing with any of the same issues today as yesterday? What can you do about this?
<--- Score

4. Who needs to know about Business Model Innovation?
<--- Score

5. Whom do you really need or want to serve?
<--- Score

6. Are there Business Model Innovation problems defined?
<--- Score

7. Have you identified your Business Model Innovation key performance indicators?
<--- Score

8. How do you identify the kinds of information that you will need?
<--- Score

9. Will a response program recognize when a crisis occurs and provide some level of response?
<--- Score

10. Consider your own Business Model Innovation project, what types of organizational problems do you think might be causing or affecting your problem, based on the work done so far?
<--- Score

11. What are the timeframes required to resolve each of the issues/problems?
<--- Score

12. How do you assess your Business Model Innovation workforce capability and capacity needs,

including skills, competencies, and staffing levels?
<--- Score

13. How do you recognize an objection?
<--- Score

14. Does your organization need more Business
Model Innovation education?
<--- Score

15. Does the problem have ethical dimensions?
<--- Score

16. What Business Model Innovation coordination do
you need?
<--- Score

17. What do you need to start doing?
<--- Score

18. What problems are you facing and how do you
consider Business Model Innovation will circumvent
those obstacles?
<--- Score

19. As a sponsor, customer or management, how
important is it to meet goals, objectives?
<--- Score

20. How much are sponsors, customers, partners,
stakeholders involved in Business Model Innovation?
In other words, what are the risks, if Business Model
Innovation does not deliver successfully?
<--- Score

21. Are your goals realistic? Do you need to redefine

your problem? Perhaps the problem has changed or maybe you have reached your goal and need to set a new one?

<--- Score

22. Who needs budgets?

<--- Score

23. Where is training needed?

<--- Score

24. To what extent does each concerned units management team recognize Business Model Innovation as an effective investment?

<--- Score

25. What is the Business Model Innovation problem definition? What do you need to resolve?

<--- Score

26. What are the Business Model Innovation resources needed?

<--- Score

27. Who needs what information?

<--- Score

28. What are your needs in relation to Business Model Innovation skills, labor, equipment, and markets?

<--- Score

29. Who needs to know?

<--- Score

30. How are the Business Model Innovation's objectives aligned to the group's overall stakeholder

strategy?
<--- Score

31. Is the quality assurance team identified?
<--- Score

32. Can management personnel recognize the monetary benefit of Business Model Innovation?
<--- Score

33. Will Business Model Innovation deliverables need to be tested and, if so, by whom?
<--- Score

34. What is the problem and/or vulnerability?
<--- Score

35. What training and capacity building actions are needed to implement proposed reforms?
<--- Score

36. Are controls defined to recognize and contain problems?
<--- Score

37. Where do you need to exercise leadership?
<--- Score

38. What situation(s) led to this Business Model Innovation Self Assessment?
<--- Score

39. Are there any specific expectations or concerns about the Business Model Innovation team, Business Model Innovation itself?
<--- Score

40. Are problem definition and motivation clearly presented?
<--- Score

41. What is the recognized need?
<--- Score

42. What are the stakeholder objectives to be achieved with Business Model Innovation?
<--- Score

43. How many trainings, in total, are needed?
<--- Score

44. How do you recognize an Business Model Innovation objection?
<--- Score

45. Think about the people you identified for your Business Model Innovation project and the project responsibilities you would assign to them, what kind of training do you think they would need to perform these responsibilities effectively?
<--- Score

46. What would happen if Business Model Innovation weren't done?
<--- Score

47. What are the clients issues and concerns?
<--- Score

48. What do employees need in the short term?
<--- Score

49. What are the expected benefits of Business Model Innovation to the stakeholder?
<--- Score

50. What is the problem or issue?
<--- Score

51. Are there any revenue recognition issues?
<--- Score

52. What Business Model Innovation problem should be solved?
<--- Score

53. Do you need different information or graphics?
<--- Score

54. What needs to be done?
<--- Score

55. What do executives need to know about business model innovation?
<--- Score

56. What does Business Model Innovation success mean to the stakeholders?
<--- Score

57. What Business Model Innovation capabilities do you need?
<--- Score

58. How do you identify subcontractor relationships?
<--- Score

59. For your Business Model Innovation project,

identify and describe the business environment, is there more than one layer to the business environment?

<--- Score

60. What Business Model Innovation events should you attend?

<--- Score

61. Is the need for organizational change recognized?

<--- Score

62. Does Business Model Innovation create potential expectations in other areas that need to be recognized and considered?

<--- Score

63. Which issues are too important to ignore?

<--- Score

64. What prevents you from making the changes you know will make you a more effective Business Model Innovation leader?

<--- Score

65. Which needs are not included or involved?

<--- Score

66. Do you have/need 24-hour access to key personnel?

<--- Score

67. Why the need?

<--- Score

68. What activities does the governance board need

to consider?
<--- Score

69. Did you miss any major Business Model Innovation issues?
<--- Score

70. Are there regulatory / compliance issues?
<--- Score

71. Who are your key stakeholders who need to sign off?
<--- Score

72. Which information does the Business Model Innovation business case need to include?
<--- Score

73. How does it fit into your organizational needs and tasks?
<--- Score

74. Would you recognize a threat from the inside?
<--- Score

75. Will it solve real problems?
<--- Score

76. Do you recognize Business Model Innovation achievements?
<--- Score

77. What creative shifts do you need to take?
<--- Score

78. Will new equipment/products be required to

facilitate Business Model Innovation delivery, for example is new software needed?
<--- Score

79. Looking at each person individually – does every one have the qualities which are needed to work in this group?
<--- Score

80. Is it needed?
<--- Score

81. Are employees recognized for desired behaviors?
<--- Score

82. What vendors make products that address the Business Model Innovation needs?
<--- Score

83. What tools and technologies are needed for a custom Business Model Innovation project?
<--- Score

84. What is the extent or complexity of the Business Model Innovation problem?
<--- Score

85. What is the smallest subset of the problem you can usefully solve?
<--- Score

86. Who should resolve the Business Model Innovation issues?
<--- Score

87. What resources or support might you need?

<--- Score

88. Who else hopes to benefit from it?
<--- Score

89. What needs to stay?
<--- Score

90. To what extent would your organization benefit from being recognized as a award recipient?
<--- Score

91. How can auditing be a preventative security measure?
<--- Score

92. What should be considered when identifying available resources, constraints, and deadlines?
<--- Score

93. Are losses recognized in a timely manner?
<--- Score

94. Are there recognized Business Model Innovation problems?
<--- Score

95. What are the minority interests and what amount of minority interests can be recognized?
<--- Score

96. Is it clear when you think of the day ahead of you what activities and tasks you need to complete?
<--- Score

97. Are employees recognized or rewarded for

performance that demonstrates the highest levels of integrity?
<--- Score

98. How are you going to measure success?
<--- Score

Add up total points for this section:
_____ = Total points for this section

Divided by: _____ (number of statements answered) = _____
Average score for this section

Transfer your score to the Business Model Innovation Index at the beginning of the Self-Assessment.

CRITERION #2: DEFINE:

INTENT: Formulate the stakeholder problem. Define the problem, needs and objectives.

In my belief, the answer to this question is clearly defined:

5 Strongly Agree

4 Agree

3 Neutral

2 Disagree

1 Strongly Disagree

1. How would you define Business Model Innovation leadership?
<--- Score

2. How do you gather Business Model Innovation requirements?
<--- Score

3. What Business Model Innovation requirements

should be gathered?
<--- Score

4. What are the rough order estimates on cost savings/
opportunities that Business Model Innovation brings?
<--- Score

5. Is the work to date meeting requirements?
<--- Score

6. What sources do you use to gather information for a
Business Model Innovation study?
<--- Score

7. Is there a clear Business Model Innovation case
definition?
<--- Score

8. When is/was the Business Model Innovation start
date?
<--- Score

9. What scope do you want your strategy to cover?
<--- Score

10. Has the direction changed at all during the course
of Business Model Innovation? If so, when did it
change and why?
<--- Score

11. How do you gather the stories?
<--- Score

12. The political context: who holds power?
<--- Score

13. What gets examined?
<--- Score

14. What are the record-keeping requirements of Business Model Innovation activities?
<--- Score

15. Has a team charter been developed and communicated?
<--- Score

16. Is the Business Model Innovation scope complete and appropriately sized?
<--- Score

17. How was the 'as is' process map developed, reviewed, verified and validated?
<--- Score

18. Will a Business Model Innovation production readiness review be required?
<--- Score

19. Scope of sensitive information?
<--- Score

20. How is the team tracking and documenting its work?
<--- Score

21. What was the context?
<--- Score

22. Is special Business Model Innovation user knowledge required?
<--- Score

23. Is there a completed SIPOC representation, describing the Suppliers, Inputs, Process, Outputs, and Customers?
<--- Score

24. Are there different segments of customers?
<--- Score

25. How do you keep key subject matter experts in the loop?
<--- Score

26. What is the definition of success?
<--- Score

27. What defines best in class?
<--- Score

28. Is there regularly 100% attendance at the team meetings? If not, have appointed substitutes attended to preserve cross-functionality and full representation?
<--- Score

29. Who defines (or who defined) the rules and roles?
<--- Score

30. Is there a Business Model Innovation management charter, including stakeholder case, problem and goal statements, scope, milestones, roles and responsibilities, communication plan?
<--- Score

31. What Business Model Innovation services do you require?

<--- Score

32. What are the boundaries of the scope? What is in bounds and what is not? What is the start point? What is the stop point?
<--- Score

33. Are task requirements clearly defined?
<--- Score

34. Do you have a Business Model Innovation success story or case study ready to tell and share?
<--- Score

35. How and when will the baselines be defined?
<--- Score

36. Who is gathering information?
<--- Score

37. What is in scope?
<--- Score

38. What is a worst-case scenario for losses?
<--- Score

39. Are required metrics defined, what are they?
<--- Score

40. What information should you gather?
<--- Score

41. How did the Business Model Innovation manager receive input to the development of a Business Model Innovation improvement plan and the estimated completion dates/times of each activity?

<--- Score

42. What is the worst case scenario?
<--- Score

43. Do you all define Business Model Innovation in the same way?
<--- Score

44. How would you define the culture at your organization, how susceptible is it to Business Model Innovation changes?
<--- Score

45. When are meeting minutes sent out? Who is on the distribution list?
<--- Score

46. Have all of the relationships been defined properly?
<--- Score

47. Is the Business Model Innovation scope manageable?
<--- Score

48. Have specific policy objectives been defined?
<--- Score

49. What is the context?
<--- Score

50. How do you manage unclear Business Model Innovation requirements?
<--- Score

51. What is out-of-scope initially?
<--- Score

52. Does the scope remain the same?
<--- Score

53. How will variation in the actual durations of each activity be dealt with to ensure that the expected Business Model Innovation results are met?
<--- Score

54. What is the scope of the Business Model Innovation work?
<--- Score

55. Is Business Model Innovation currently on schedule according to the plan?
<--- Score

56. Are all requirements met?
<--- Score

57. Has/have the customer(s) been identified?
<--- Score

58. What is the scope?
<--- Score

59. What are the dynamics of the communication plan?
<--- Score

60. How do you hand over Business Model Innovation context?
<--- Score

61. Where can you gather more information?
<--- Score

62. What are the Business Model Innovation use cases?
<--- Score

63. How do you manage scope?
<--- Score

64. Is Business Model Innovation linked to key stakeholder goals and objectives?
<--- Score

65. Has a project plan, Gantt chart, or similar been developed/completed?
<--- Score

66. Do you have organizational privacy requirements?
<--- Score

67. How have you defined all Business Model Innovation requirements first?
<--- Score

68. What information do you gather?
<--- Score

69. Is the improvement team aware of the different versions of a process: what they think it is vs. what it actually is vs. what it should be vs. what it could be?
<--- Score

70. How do you gather requirements?
<--- Score

71. What is in the scope and what is not in scope?
<--- Score

72. Is the scope of Business Model Innovation defined?
<--- Score

73. If substitutes have been appointed, have they been briefed on the Business Model Innovation goals and received regular communications as to the progress to date?
<--- Score

74. Are different versions of process maps needed to account for the different types of inputs?
<--- Score

75. Are there any constraints known that bear on the ability to perform Business Model Innovation work? How is the team addressing them?
<--- Score

76. Is there a completed, verified, and validated high-level 'as is' (not 'should be' or 'could be') stakeholder process map?
<--- Score

77. What are the requirements for audit information?
<--- Score

78. Are approval levels defined for contracts and supplements to contracts?
<--- Score

79. How can the value of Business Model Innovation be defined?

<--- Score

80. What knowledge or experience is required?
<--- Score

81. Who is gathering Business Model Innovation information?
<--- Score

82. How will the Business Model Innovation team and the group measure complete success of Business Model Innovation?
<--- Score

83. Has your scope been defined?
<--- Score

84. Do the problem and goal statements meet the SMART criteria (specific, measurable, attainable, relevant, and time-bound)?
<--- Score

85. Has the Business Model Innovation work been fairly and/or equitably divided and delegated among team members who are qualified and capable to perform the work? Has everyone contributed?
<--- Score

86. How are consistent Business Model Innovation definitions important?
<--- Score

87. What are the tasks and definitions?
<--- Score

88. What scope to assess?

<--- Score

89. Are accountability and ownership for Business Model Innovation clearly defined?
<--- Score

90. Has the improvement team collected the 'voice of the customer' (obtained feedback – qualitative and quantitative)?
<--- Score

91. What system do you use for gathering Business Model Innovation information?
<--- Score

92. Is the current 'as is' process being followed? If not, what are the discrepancies?
<--- Score

93. Is the team adequately staffed with the desired cross-functionality? If not, what additional resources are available to the team?
<--- Score

94. Has everyone on the team, including the team leaders, been properly trained?
<--- Score

95. What are the Roles and Responsibilities for each team member and its leadership? Where is this documented?
<--- Score

96. How often are the team meetings?
<--- Score

97. How do you manage changes in Business Model Innovation requirements?
<--- Score

98. Is there a critical path to deliver Business Model Innovation results?
<--- Score

99. How does the Business Model Innovation manager ensure against scope creep?
<--- Score

100. What is the definition of Business Model Innovation excellence?
<--- Score

101. When is the estimated completion date?
<--- Score

102. Has a Business Model Innovation requirement not been met?
<--- Score

103. Does the team have regular meetings?
<--- Score

104. Why are you doing Business Model Innovation and what is the scope?
<--- Score

105. In what way can you redefine the criteria of choice clients have in your category in your favor?
<--- Score

106. What constraints exist that might impact the team?

<--- Score

107. Are roles and responsibilities formally defined?
<--- Score

108. What critical content must be communicated –
who, what, when, where, and how?
<--- Score

109. What customer feedback methods were used to
solicit their input?
<--- Score

110. What specifically is the problem? Where does it
occur? When does it occur? What is its extent?
<--- Score

111. Is scope creep really all bad news?
<--- Score

112. What are the core elements of the Business
Model Innovation business case?
<--- Score

113. What is out of scope?
<--- Score

114. Has anyone else (internal or external to the
group) attempted to solve this problem or a similar
one before? If so, what knowledge can be leveraged
from these previous efforts?
<--- Score

115. What key stakeholder process output measure(s)
does Business Model Innovation leverage and how?
<--- Score

116. Are the Business Model Innovation requirements testable?

<--- Score

117. What are the Business Model Innovation tasks and definitions?

<--- Score

118. What baselines are required to be defined and managed?

<--- Score

119. Are resources adequate for the scope?

<--- Score

120. Who are the Business Model Innovation improvement team members, including Management Leads and Coaches?

<--- Score

121. Have all basic functions of Business Model Innovation been defined?

<--- Score

122. What is the scope of the Business Model Innovation effort?

<--- Score

123. Has a high-level 'as is' process map been completed, verified and validated?

<--- Score

124. Are audit criteria, scope, frequency and methods defined?

<--- Score

125. Is it clearly defined in and to your organization what you do?
<--- Score

126. What intelligence can you gather?
<--- Score

127. What is the scope of Business Model Innovation?
<--- Score

128. How do you think the partners involved in Business Model Innovation would have defined success?
<--- Score

129. Have the customer needs been translated into specific, measurable requirements? How?
<--- Score

130. What are the compelling stakeholder reasons for embarking on Business Model Innovation?
<--- Score

131. What are (control) requirements for Business Model Innovation Information?
<--- Score

132. Are the Business Model Innovation requirements complete?
<--- Score

133. What would be the goal or target for a Business Model Innovation's improvement team?
<--- Score

Add up total points for this section:
_____ = Total points for this section

Divided by: _____ (number of
statements answered) = _____
Average score for this section

Transfer your score to the Business
Model Innovation Index at the beginning
of the Self-Assessment.

CRITERION #3: MEASURE:

INTENT: Gather the correct data.
Measure the current performance and
evolution of the situation.

In my belief, the answer to this
question is clearly defined:

5 Strongly Agree

4 Agree

3 Neutral

2 Disagree

1 Strongly Disagree

1. Have design-to-cost goals been established?
<--- Score

2. What is the cause of any Business Model Innovation gaps?
<--- Score

3. How do you aggregate measures across priorities?
<--- Score

4. How are costs allocated?
<--- Score

5. How will success or failure be measured?
<--- Score

6. How do you measure success?
<--- Score

7. Have you included everything in your Business Model Innovation cost models?
<--- Score

8. How do you verify the Business Model Innovation requirements quality?
<--- Score

9. What tests verify requirements?
<--- Score

10. What are your operating costs?
<--- Score

11. Was a business case (cost/benefit) developed?
<--- Score

12. How do you measure lifecycle phases?
<--- Score

13. What are you verifying?
<--- Score

14. What are the operational costs after Business Model Innovation deployment?
<--- Score

15. How long to keep data and how to manage retention costs?

<--- Score

16. Is it possible to estimate the impact of unanticipated complexity such as wrong or failed assumptions, feedback, etcetera on proposed reforms?

<--- Score

17. What is your Business Model Innovation quality cost segregation study?

<--- Score

18. Are there any easy-to-implement alternatives to Business Model Innovation? Sometimes other solutions are available that do not require the cost implications of a full-blown project?

<--- Score

19. Does the Business Model Innovation task fit the client's priorities?

<--- Score

20. What are allowable costs?

<--- Score

21. What would it cost to replace your technology?

<--- Score

22. How can you reduce the costs of obtaining inputs?

<--- Score

23. What happens if cost savings do not materialize?

<--- Score

24. Does a Business Model Innovation quantification method exist?
<--- Score

25. Do the benefits outweigh the costs?
<--- Score

26. How do you verify and develop ideas and innovations?
<--- Score

27. What does losing customers cost your organization?
<--- Score

28. How will measures be used to manage and adapt?
<--- Score

29. What are the costs of reform?
<--- Score

30. What are the costs?
<--- Score

31. Are the Business Model Innovation benefits worth its costs?
<--- Score

32. How do you measure variability?
<--- Score

33. Which measures and indicators matter?
<--- Score

34. How do you measure efficient delivery of Business

Model Innovation services?
<--- Score

35. What are the strategic priorities for this year?
<--- Score

36. What can be used to verify compliance?
<--- Score

37. How do you control the overall costs of your work processes?
<--- Score

38. What could cause delays in the schedule?
<--- Score

39. What does a Test Case verify?
<--- Score

40. How will you measure success?
<--- Score

41. Do you verify that corrective actions were taken?
<--- Score

42. What methods are feasible and acceptable to estimate the impact of reforms?
<--- Score

43. How is performance measured?
<--- Score

44. Which costs should be taken into account?
<--- Score

45. How do you quantify and qualify impacts?

<--- Score

46. How to cause the change?
<--- Score

47. How can you measure Business Model Innovation in a systematic way?
<--- Score

48. Are actual costs in line with budgeted costs?
<--- Score

49. Are there measurements based on task performance?
<--- Score

50. What causes innovation to fail or succeed in your organization?
<--- Score

51. What is the total fixed cost?
<--- Score

52. What details are required of the Business Model Innovation cost structure?
<--- Score

53. Do you have an issue in getting priority?
<--- Score

54. What harm might be caused?
<--- Score

55. What disadvantage does this cause for the user?
<--- Score

56. What does your operating model cost?
<--- Score

57. What are the uncertainties surrounding estimates of impact?
<--- Score

58. Are you able to realize any cost savings?
<--- Score

59. How do you verify your resources?
<--- Score

60. What is the total cost related to deploying Business Model Innovation, including any consulting or professional services?
<--- Score

61. What are the Business Model Innovation key cost drivers?
<--- Score

62. What are the types and number of measures to use?
<--- Score

63. Did you tackle the cause or the symptom?
<--- Score

64. How do you verify the authenticity of the data and information used?
<--- Score

65. Where is the cost?
<--- Score

66. What causes extra work or rework?
<--- Score

67. Where is it measured?
<--- Score

68. How are measurements made?
<--- Score

69. Does management have the right priorities among projects?
<--- Score

70. How will costs be allocated?
<--- Score

71. How is the value delivered by Business Model Innovation being measured?
<--- Score

72. How will effects be measured?
<--- Score

73. Do you effectively measure and reward individual and team performance?
<--- Score

74. What users will be impacted?
<--- Score

75. When should you bother with diagrams?
<--- Score

76. Is the cost worth the Business Model Innovation effort ?
<--- Score

77. How sensitive must the Business Model Innovation strategy be to cost?
<--- Score

78. What is the Business Model Innovation business impact?
<--- Score

79. What are the costs of delaying Business Model Innovation action?
<--- Score

80. When a disaster occurs, who gets priority?
<--- Score

81. What could cause you to change course?
<--- Score

82. What are the estimated costs of proposed changes?
<--- Score

83. Do you have a flow diagram of what happens?
<--- Score

84. What are hidden Business Model Innovation quality costs?
<--- Score

85. What are the current costs of the Business Model Innovation process?
<--- Score

86. How do you verify if Business Model Innovation is built right?

<--- Score

87. How do you verify and validate the Business Model Innovation data?
<--- Score

88. Where can you go to verify the info?
<--- Score

89. How frequently do you track Business Model Innovation measures?
<--- Score

90. How can you manage cost down?
<--- Score

91. Are the measurements objective?
<--- Score

92. What is your decision requirements diagram?
<--- Score

93. Are supply costs steady or fluctuating?
<--- Score

94. What is the cost of rework?
<--- Score

95. What is an unallowable cost?
<--- Score

96. What relevant entities could be measured?
<--- Score

97. Are there competing Business Model Innovation priorities?

<--- Score

98. Is there an opportunity to verify requirements?
<--- Score

99. Are Business Model Innovation vulnerabilities categorized and prioritized?
<--- Score

100. Has a cost center been established?
<--- Score

101. What are the costs and benefits?
<--- Score

102. What do people want to verify?
<--- Score

103. What would be a real cause for concern?
<--- Score

104. Who should receive measurement reports?
<--- Score

105. Are the units of measure consistent?
<--- Score

106. Among the Business Model Innovation product and service cost to be estimated, which is considered hardest to estimate?
<--- Score

107. Do you aggressively reward and promote the people who have the biggest impact on creating excellent Business Model Innovation services/products?

<--- Score

108. At what cost?
<--- Score

109. How will your organization measure success?
<--- Score

110. Who is involved in verifying compliance?
<--- Score

111. Are you aware of what could cause a problem?
<--- Score

112. Which Business Model Innovation impacts are significant?
<--- Score

113. What causes investor action?
<--- Score

114. How do your measurements capture actionable Business Model Innovation information for use in exceeding your customers expectations and securing your customers engagement?
<--- Score

115. Is the solution cost-effective?
<--- Score

116. Are you taking your company in the direction of better and revenue or cheaper and cost?
<--- Score

117. Who pays the cost?
<--- Score

118. What do you measure and why?
<--- Score

119. How can you reduce costs?
<--- Score

120. How can you measure the performance?
<--- Score

121. Have you made assumptions about the shape of the future, particularly its impact on your customers and competitors?
<--- Score

122. How do you verify performance?
<--- Score

123. How can a Business Model Innovation test verify your ideas or assumptions?
<--- Score

124. Are indirect costs charged to the Business Model Innovation program?
<--- Score

125. What is measured? Why?
<--- Score

126. How is progress measured?
<--- Score

127. What are the Business Model Innovation investment costs?
<--- Score

128. What evidence is there and what is measured?
<--- Score

129. When are costs are incurred?
<--- Score

130. What are your primary costs, revenues, assets?
<--- Score

131. What are your key Business Model Innovation organizational performance measures, including key short and longer-term financial measures?
<--- Score

132. What are your customers expectations and measures?
<--- Score

133. How will you measure your Business Model Innovation effectiveness?
<--- Score

134. What measurements are being captured?
<--- Score

Add up total points for this section:
_____ = Total points for this section

Divided by: _____ (number of statements answered) = _____
Average score for this section

Transfer your score to the Business Model Innovation Index at the beginning of the Self-Assessment.

CRITERION #4: ANALYZE:

INTENT: Analyze causes, assumptions and hypotheses.

In my belief, the answer to this question is clearly defined:

5 Strongly Agree

4 Agree

3 Neutral

2 Disagree

1 Strongly Disagree

1. Are gaps between current performance and the goal performance identified?
<--- Score

2. Has data output been validated?
<--- Score

3. How does business model innovation process happen within your organization?
<--- Score

4. How do you identify specific Business Model Innovation investment opportunities and emerging trends?
<--- Score

5. What controls do you have in place to protect data?
<--- Score

6. How is data used for program management and improvement?
<--- Score

7. What are the best opportunities for value improvement?
<--- Score

8. Do quality systems drive continuous improvement?
<--- Score

9. Were Pareto charts (or similar) used to portray the 'heavy hitters' (or key sources of variation)?
<--- Score

10. What are the Business Model Innovation design outputs?
<--- Score

11. Were there any improvement opportunities identified from the process analysis?
<--- Score

12. Who gets your output?
<--- Score

13. What qualifications are necessary?

<--- Score

14. Is the final output clearly identified?
<--- Score

15. How do you ensure that the Business Model Innovation opportunity is realistic?
<--- Score

16. Is the gap/opportunity displayed and communicated in financial terms?
<--- Score

17. What are your Business Model Innovation processes?
<--- Score

18. Have any additional benefits been identified that will result from closing all or most of the gaps?
<--- Score

19. Do you, as a leader, bounce back quickly from setbacks?
<--- Score

20. Where is the data coming from to measure compliance?
<--- Score

21. How is the way you as the leader think and process information affecting your organizational culture?
<--- Score

22. Is data and process analysis, root cause analysis and quantifying the gap/opportunity in place?
<--- Score

23. What Business Model Innovation data will be collected?

<--- Score

24. What Business Model Innovation data do you gather or use now?

<--- Score

25. What qualifications are needed?

<--- Score

26. Do you understand your management processes today?

<--- Score

27. What Business Model Innovation data should be managed?

<--- Score

28. What is the output?

<--- Score

29. What are your key performance measures or indicators and in-process measures for the control and improvement of your Business Model Innovation processes?

<--- Score

30. Who will gather what data?

<--- Score

31. How does the organization define, manage, and improve its Business Model Innovation processes?

<--- Score

32. How often will data be collected for measures?
<--- Score

33. How was the detailed process map generated, verified, and validated?
<--- Score

34. What Business Model Innovation data should be collected?
<--- Score

35. What is the complexity of the output produced?
<--- Score

36. Who qualifies to gain access to data?
<--- Score

37. What tools were used to narrow the list of possible causes?
<--- Score

38. Think about some of the processes you undertake within your organization, which do you own?
<--- Score

39. Do staff qualifications match your project?
<--- Score

40. How will corresponding data be collected?
<--- Score

41. What does the data say about the performance of the stakeholder process?
<--- Score

42. How has the Business Model Innovation data been

gathered?
<--- Score

43. How do you use Business Model Innovation data and information to support organizational decision making and innovation?
<--- Score

44. What is your organizations system for selecting qualified vendors?
<--- Score

45. How do you measure the operational performance of your key work systems and processes, including productivity, cycle time, and other appropriate measures of process effectiveness, efficiency, and innovation?
<--- Score

46. Is there a strict change management process?
<--- Score

47. What tools were used to generate the list of possible causes?
<--- Score

48. What qualifications and skills do you need?
<--- Score

49. What types of data do your Business Model Innovation indicators require?
<--- Score

50. Is there any way to speed up the process?
<--- Score

51. What are evaluation criteria for the output?
<--- Score

52. What is the oversight process?
<--- Score

53. How is the data gathered?
<--- Score

54. Do several people in different organizational units assist with the Business Model Innovation process?
<--- Score

55. What do you need to qualify?
<--- Score

56. Is the required Business Model Innovation data gathered?
<--- Score

57. What internal processes need improvement?
<--- Score

58. Who is involved in the management review process?
<--- Score

59. What Business Model Innovation metrics are outputs of the process?
<--- Score

60. Did any value-added analysis or 'lean thinking' take place to identify some of the gaps shown on the 'as is' process map?
<--- Score

61. How much data can be collected in the given timeframe?
<--- Score

62. What kind of crime could a potential new hire have committed that would not only not disqualify him/her from being hired by your organization, but would actually indicate that he/she might be a particularly good fit?
<--- Score

63. Are your outputs consistent?
<--- Score

64. How will the data be checked for quality?
<--- Score

65. What is the cost of poor quality as supported by the team's analysis?
<--- Score

66. What successful thing are you doing today that may be blinding you to new growth opportunities?
<--- Score

67. Did any additional data need to be collected?
<--- Score

68. What is the Value Stream Mapping?
<--- Score

69. What systems/processes must you excel at?
<--- Score

70. What are the processes for audit reporting and management?

<--- Score

71. Think about the functions involved in your Business Model Innovation project, what processes flow from these functions?
<--- Score

72. Which Business Model Innovation data should be retained?
<--- Score

73. Are all team members qualified for all tasks?
<--- Score

74. What are the Business Model Innovation business drivers?
<--- Score

75. Is the performance gap determined?
<--- Score

76. A compounding model resolution with available relevant data can often provide insight towards a solution methodology; which Business Model Innovation models, tools and techniques are necessary?
<--- Score

77. Are you missing Business Model Innovation opportunities?
<--- Score

78. Who will facilitate the team and process?
<--- Score

79. Identify an operational issue in your organization,

for example, could a particular task be done more quickly or more efficiently by Business Model Innovation?

<--- Score

80. Is the Business Model Innovation process severely broken such that a re-design is necessary?

<--- Score

81. Who is involved with workflow mapping?

<--- Score

82. Were any designed experiments used to generate additional insight into the data analysis?

<--- Score

83. Who owns what data?

<--- Score

84. Have you defined which data is gathered how?

<--- Score

85. How will the change process be managed?

<--- Score

86. Should you invest in industry-recognized qualifications?

<--- Score

87. Do your leaders quickly bounce back from setbacks?

<--- Score

88. Can you add value to the current Business Model Innovation decision-making process (largely qualitative) by incorporating uncertainty modeling

(more quantitative)?

<--- Score

89. What are the personnel training and qualifications required?

<--- Score

90. What process should you select for improvement?

<--- Score

91. Where is Business Model Innovation data gathered?

<--- Score

92. How can risk management be tied procedurally to process elements?

<--- Score

93. What will drive Business Model Innovation change?

<--- Score

94. What quality tools were used to get through the analyze phase?

<--- Score

95. What qualifications do Business Model Innovation leaders need?

<--- Score

96. Was a detailed process map created to amplify critical steps of the 'as is' stakeholder process?

<--- Score

97. How is the Business Model Innovation Value Stream Mapping managed?

<--- Score

98. Have the problem and goal statements been updated to reflect the additional knowledge gained from the analyze phase?
<--- Score

99. Do you have the authority to produce the output?
<--- Score

100. What data is gathered?
<--- Score

101. How are outputs preserved and protected?
<--- Score

102. Record-keeping requirements flow from the records needed as inputs, outputs, controls and for transformation of a Business Model Innovation process, are the records needed as inputs to the Business Model Innovation process available?
<--- Score

103. How is Business Model Innovation data gathered?
<--- Score

104. An organizationally feasible system request is one that considers the mission, goals and objectives of the organization, key questions are: is the Business Model Innovation solution request practical and will it solve a problem or take advantage of an opportunity to achieve company goals?
<--- Score

105. What are the disruptive Business Model

Innovation technologies that enable your organization to radically change your business processes?

<--- Score

106. Has an output goal been set?

<--- Score

107. Is there an established change management process?

<--- Score

108. How will the Business Model Innovation data be captured?

<--- Score

109. What were the financial benefits resulting from any 'ground fruit or low-hanging fruit' (quick fixes)?

<--- Score

110. How do your work systems and key work processes relate to and capitalize on your core competencies?

<--- Score

111. What is the Business Model Innovation Driver?

<--- Score

112. What did the team gain from developing a sub-process map?

<--- Score

113. How do you implement and manage your work processes to ensure that they meet design requirements?

<--- Score

114. Is the suppliers process defined and controlled?
<--- Score

115. What is your organizations process which leads to recognition of value generation?
<--- Score

116. What output to create?
<--- Score

117. What conclusions were drawn from the team's data collection and analysis? How did the team reach these conclusions?
<--- Score

118. How do you define collaboration and team output?
<--- Score

119. When should a process be art not science?
<--- Score

120. Are all staff in core Business Model Innovation subjects Highly Qualified?
<--- Score

121. Was a cause-and-effect diagram used to explore the different types of causes (or sources of variation)?
<--- Score

122. How difficult is it to qualify what Business Model Innovation ROI is?
<--- Score

123. What training and qualifications will you need?

<--- Score

124. What are your best practices for minimizing Business Model Innovation project risk, while demonstrating incremental value and quick wins throughout the Business Model Innovation project lifecycle?
<--- Score

125. What are your outputs?
<--- Score

126. What were the crucial 'moments of truth' on the process map?
<--- Score

127. What are your current levels and trends in key measures or indicators of Business Model Innovation product and process performance that are important to and directly serve your customers? How do these results compare with the performance of your competitors and other organizations with similar offerings?
<--- Score

128. Where can you get qualified talent today?
<--- Score

129. What are the necessary qualifications?
<--- Score

130. What resources go in to get the desired output?
<--- Score

131. Is pre-qualification of suppliers carried out?
<--- Score

132. What qualifies as competition?
<--- Score

133. What process improvements will be needed?
<--- Score

134. What are the revised rough estimates of the financial savings/opportunity for Business Model Innovation improvements?
<--- Score

135. What information qualified as important?
<--- Score

136. What, related to, Business Model Innovation processes does your organization outsource?
<--- Score

Add up total points for this section:
_____ = Total points for this section

Divided by: _____ (number of statements answered) = _____
Average score for this section

Transfer your score to the Business Model Innovation Index at the beginning of the Self-Assessment.

CRITERION #5: IMPROVE:

INTENT: Develop a practical solution. Innovate, establish and test the solution and to measure the results.

In my belief, the answer to this question is clearly defined:

5 Strongly Agree

4 Agree

3 Neutral

2 Disagree

1 Strongly Disagree

1. Do vendor agreements bring new compliance risk ?
<--- Score

2. Are events managed to resolution?
<--- Score

3. What actually has to improve and by how much?
<--- Score

4. How do you manage and improve your Business Model Innovation work systems to deliver customer value and achieve organizational success and sustainability?
<--- Score

5. What are the implications of the one critical Business Model Innovation decision 10 minutes, 10 months, and 10 years from now?
<--- Score

6. How are Business Model Innovation risks managed?
<--- Score

7. What is the magnitude of the improvements?
<--- Score

8. What improvements have been achieved?
<--- Score

9. Who controls the risk?
<--- Score

10. Who will be responsible for documenting the Business Model Innovation requirements in detail?
<--- Score

11. What does the 'should be' process map/design look like?
<--- Score

12. How will you know that a change is an improvement?
<--- Score

13. Which Business Model Innovation solution is

appropriate?
<--- Score

14. Do you have the optimal project management team structure?
<--- Score

15. Is risk periodically assessed?
<--- Score

16. How will you know when its improved?
<--- Score

17. What risks do you need to manage?
<--- Score

18. What criteria will you use to assess your Business Model Innovation risks?
<--- Score

19. Who makes the Business Model Innovation decisions in your organization?
<--- Score

20. How can you improve Business Model Innovation?
<--- Score

21. What tools were used to evaluate the potential solutions?
<--- Score

22. What is the implementation plan?
<--- Score

23. How does your organization evaluate strategic Business Model Innovation success?

<--- Score

24. For decision problems, how do you develop a decision statement?
<--- Score

25. What were the underlying assumptions on the cost-benefit analysis?
<--- Score

26. What are your current levels and trends in key measures or indicators of workforce and leader development?
<--- Score

27. Will the controls trigger any other risks?
<--- Score

28. Do you cover the five essential competencies: Communication, Collaboration,Innovation, Adaptability, and Leadership that improve an organizations ability to leverage the new Business Model Innovation in a volatile global economy?
<--- Score

29. What attendant changes will need to be made to ensure that the solution is successful?
<--- Score

30. How do you manage Business Model Innovation risk?
<--- Score

31. Was a Business Model Innovation charter developed?
<--- Score

32. What tools were used to tap into the creativity and encourage 'outside the box' thinking?
<--- Score

33. Are the risks fully understood, reasonable and manageable?
<--- Score

34. What strategies for Business Model Innovation improvement are successful?
<--- Score

35. How are policy decisions made and where?
<--- Score

36. Is Business Model Innovation documentation maintained?
<--- Score

37. How do you improve Business Model Innovation service perception, and satisfaction?
<--- Score

38. What assumptions are made about the solution and approach?
<--- Score

39. Is there a small-scale pilot for proposed improvement(s)? What conclusions were drawn from the outcomes of a pilot?
<--- Score

40. What resources are required for the improvement efforts?
<--- Score

41. Why improve in the first place?
<--- Score

42. What needs improvement? Why?
<--- Score

43. Is there a high likelihood that any recommendations will achieve their intended results?
<--- Score

44. Which of the recognised risks out of all risks can be most likely transferred?
<--- Score

45. How do you keep improving Business Model Innovation?
<--- Score

46. Who are the key stakeholders for the Business Model Innovation evaluation?
<--- Score

47. Who are the people involved in developing and implementing Business Model Innovation?
<--- Score

48. What went well, what should change, what can improve?
<--- Score

49. Are you assessing Business Model Innovation and risk?
<--- Score

50. How do you improve your likelihood of success ?

<--- Score

51. Is any Business Model Innovation documentation required?
<--- Score

52. How do you measure improved Business Model Innovation service perception, and satisfaction?
<--- Score

53. When you map the key players in your own work and the types/domains of relationships with them, which relationships do you find easy and which challenging, and why?
<--- Score

54. Risk factors: what are the characteristics of Business Model Innovation that make it risky?
<--- Score

55. What practices helps your organization to develop its capacity to recognize patterns?
<--- Score

56. Have you identified breakpoints and/or risk tolerances that will trigger broad consideration of a potential need for intervention or modification of strategy?
<--- Score

57. How can skill-level changes improve Business Model Innovation?
<--- Score

58. Who are the Business Model Innovation decision-makers?

<--- Score

59. Are risk management tasks balanced centrally and locally?
<--- Score

60. Is the solution technically practical?
<--- Score

61. How will you measure the results?
<--- Score

62. How risky is your organization?
<--- Score

63. What tools were most useful during the improve phase?
<--- Score

64. How does the team improve its work?
<--- Score

65. Would you develop a Business Model Innovation Communication Strategy?
<--- Score

66. How will you recognize and celebrate results?
<--- Score

67. Risk Identification: What are the possible risk events your organization faces in relation to Business Model Innovation?
<--- Score

68. What were the criteria for evaluating a Business Model Innovation pilot?

<--- Score

69. How do you go about comparing Business Model Innovation approaches/solutions?
<--- Score

70. Who manages supplier risk management in your organization?
<--- Score

71. To what extent does management recognize Business Model Innovation as a tool to increase the results?
<--- Score

72. Risk events: what are the things that could go wrong?
<--- Score

73. What are the concrete Business Model Innovation results?
<--- Score

74. Do the viable solutions scale to future needs?
<--- Score

75. Who should make the Business Model Innovation decisions?
<--- Score

76. How do you measure progress and evaluate training effectiveness?
<--- Score

77. Can the solution be designed and implemented within an acceptable time period?

<--- Score

78. How significant is the improvement in the eyes of the end user?
<--- Score

79. Who will be responsible for making the decisions to include or exclude requested changes once Business Model Innovation is underway?
<--- Score

80. How do you define the solutions' scope?
<--- Score

81. Is the Business Model Innovation documentation thorough?
<--- Score

82. What are the affordable Business Model Innovation risks?
<--- Score

83. Who manages Business Model Innovation risk?
<--- Score

84. Can you integrate quality management and risk management?
<--- Score

85. What is Business Model Innovation risk?
<--- Score

86. What lessons, if any, from a pilot were incorporated into the design of the full-scale solution?
<--- Score

87. What error proofing will be done to address some of the discrepancies observed in the 'as is' process?
<--- Score

88. What can you do to improve?
<--- Score

89. How is continuous improvement applied to risk management?
<--- Score

90. How do you link measurement and risk?
<--- Score

91. Business Model Innovation risk decisions: whose call Is It?
<--- Score

92. How can you improve performance?
<--- Score

93. How do you deal with Business Model Innovation risk?
<--- Score

94. What Business Model Innovation improvements can be made?
<--- Score

95. What do you want to improve?
<--- Score

96. If you could go back in time five years, what decision would you make differently? What is your best guess as to what decision you're making today you might regret five years from now?

<--- Score

97. For estimation problems, how do you develop an estimation statement?
<--- Score

98. What alternative responses are available to manage risk?
<--- Score

99. Does the goal represent a desired result that can be measured?
<--- Score

100. How do the Business Model Innovation results compare with the performance of your competitors and other organizations with similar offerings?
<--- Score

101. Are the key business and technology risks being managed?
<--- Score

102. What are the Business Model Innovation security risks?
<--- Score

103. Do you need to do a usability evaluation?
<--- Score

104. What to do with the results or outcomes of measurements?
<--- Score

105. How can you better manage risk?
<--- Score

106. Can you identify any significant risks or exposures to Business Model Innovation third- parties (vendors, service providers, alliance partners etc) that concern you?
<--- Score

107. At what point will vulnerability assessments be performed once Business Model Innovation is put into production (e.g., ongoing Risk Management after implementation)?
<--- Score

108. How do you decide how much to remunerate an employee?
<--- Score

109. Who are the Business Model Innovation decision makers?
<--- Score

110. Are the most efficient solutions problem-specific?
<--- Score

111. Is the measure of success for Business Model Innovation understandable to a variety of people?
<--- Score

112. Have you achieved Business Model Innovation improvements?
<--- Score

113. Where do the Business Model Innovation decisions reside?
<--- Score

114. Who do you report Business Model Innovation results to?
<--- Score

115. In the past few months, what is the smallest change you have made that has had the biggest positive result? What was it about that small change that produced the large return?
<--- Score

116. Are procedures documented for managing Business Model Innovation risks?
<--- Score

117. What area needs the greatest improvement?
<--- Score

118. Was a pilot designed for the proposed solution(s)?
<--- Score

119. How will you know that you have improved?
<--- Score

120. Do those selected for the Business Model Innovation team have a good general understanding of what Business Model Innovation is all about?
<--- Score

121. Is there any other Business Model Innovation solution?
<--- Score

122. Is the scope clearly documented?
<--- Score

123. What current systems have to be understood and/or changed?
<--- Score

124. Were any criteria developed to assist the team in testing and evaluating potential solutions?
<--- Score

125. How do you mitigate Business Model Innovation risk?
<--- Score

126. Is the Business Model Innovation risk managed?
<--- Score

127. What tools do you use once you have decided on a Business Model Innovation strategy and more importantly how do you choose?
<--- Score

128. What is Business Model Innovation's impact on utilizing the best solution(s)?
<--- Score

129. How scalable is your Business Model Innovation solution?
<--- Score

130. What is the team's contingency plan for potential problems occurring in implementation?
<--- Score

131. What are the expected Business Model Innovation results?
<--- Score

132. Who will be using the results of the measurement activities?
<--- Score

133. How do you measure risk?
<--- Score

134. Explorations of the frontiers of Business Model Innovation will help you build influence, improve Business Model Innovation, optimize decision making, and sustain change, what is your approach?
<--- Score

135. What should a proof of concept or pilot accomplish?
<--- Score

136. How is knowledge sharing about risk management improved?
<--- Score

137. Are decisions made in a timely manner?
<--- Score

138. What communications are necessary to support the implementation of the solution?
<--- Score

139. How do you improve productivity?
<--- Score

140. Is the Business Model Innovation solution sustainable?
<--- Score

141. Does a good decision guarantee a good

outcome?
<--- Score

Add up total points for this section:
_ _ _ _ _ = Total points for this section

Divided by: _ _ _ _ _ _ (number of
statements answered) = _ _ _ _ _ _
Average score for this section

Transfer your score to the Business
Model Innovation Index at the beginning
of the Self-Assessment.

CRITERION #6: CONTROL:

INTENT: Implement the practical solution. Maintain the performance and correct possible complications.

In my belief, the answer to this question is clearly defined:

5 Strongly Agree

4 Agree

3 Neutral

2 Disagree

1 Strongly Disagree

1. Is new knowledge gained imbedded in the response plan?
<--- Score

2. Have new or revised work instructions resulted?
<--- Score

3. How can you best use all of your knowledge repositories to enhance learning and sharing?

<--- Score

4. Who sets the Business Model Innovation standards?
<--- Score

5. How do senior leaders actions reflect a commitment to the organizations Business Model Innovation values?
<--- Score

6. How widespread is its use?
<--- Score

7. Is there documentation that will support the successful operation of the improvement?
<--- Score

8. What do your reports reflect?
<--- Score

9. What are you attempting to measure/monitor?
<--- Score

10. Does a troubleshooting guide exist or is it needed?
<--- Score

11. How is Business Model Innovation project cost planned, managed, monitored?
<--- Score

12. What is the standard for acceptable Business Model Innovation performance?
<--- Score

13. Act/Adjust: What Do you Need to Do Differently?
<--- Score

14. Are documented procedures clear and easy to follow for the operators?
<--- Score

15. What is your plan to assess your security risks?
<--- Score

16. What are the known security controls?
<--- Score

17. How will Business Model Innovation decisions be made and monitored?
<--- Score

18. Is a response plan established and deployed?
<--- Score

19. What key inputs and outputs are being measured on an ongoing basis?
<--- Score

20. Does the Business Model Innovation performance meet the customer's requirements?
<--- Score

21. Is the Business Model Innovation test/monitoring cost justified?
<--- Score

22. Who controls critical resources?
<--- Score

23. What do you stand for--and what are you against?
<--- Score

24. Is knowledge gained on process shared and institutionalized?
<--- Score

25. Are there documented procedures?
<--- Score

26. What Business Model Innovation standards are applicable?
<--- Score

27. Can you adapt and adjust to changing Business Model Innovation situations?
<--- Score

28. Is there a transfer of ownership and knowledge to process owner and process team tasked with the responsibilities.
<--- Score

29. Are the Business Model Innovation standards challenging?
<--- Score

30. Who is going to spread your message?
<--- Score

31. How will the process owner and team be able to hold the gains?
<--- Score

32. How might the group capture best practices and lessons learned so as to leverage improvements?
<--- Score

33. You may have created your quality measures at a

time when you lacked resources, technology wasn't up to the required standard, or low service levels were the industry norm. Have those circumstances changed?

<--- Score

34. Business model innovations for electric mobility: what can be learned from existing business model patterns?

<--- Score

35. Is there a Business Model Innovation Communication plan covering who needs to get what information when?

<--- Score

36. Do the Business Model Innovation decisions you make today help people and the planet tomorrow?

<--- Score

37. Are controls in place and consistently applied?

<--- Score

38. What should the next improvement project be that is related to Business Model Innovation?

<--- Score

39. What is the best design framework for Business Model Innovation organization now that, in a post industrial-age if the top-down, command and control model is no longer relevant?

<--- Score

40. Does job training on the documented procedures need to be part of the process team's education and training?

<--- Score

41. What is the recommended frequency of auditing?
<--- Score

42. Will any special training be provided for results interpretation?
<--- Score

43. Do you monitor the Business Model Innovation decisions made and fine tune them as they evolve?
<--- Score

44. Is there a control plan in place for sustaining improvements (short and long-term)?
<--- Score

45. Has the Business Model Innovation value of standards been quantified?
<--- Score

46. Are operating procedures consistent?
<--- Score

47. Is there an action plan in case of emergencies?
<--- Score

48. What do you measure to verify effectiveness gains?
<--- Score

49. Are new process steps, standards, and documentation ingrained into normal operations?
<--- Score

50. Are suggested corrective/restorative actions

indicated on the response plan for known causes to problems that might surface?
<--- Score

51. How will report readings be checked to effectively monitor performance?
<--- Score

52. What adjustments to the strategies are needed?
<--- Score

53. What other areas of the group might benefit from the Business Model Innovation team's improvements, knowledge, and learning?
<--- Score

54. How will the process owner verify improvement in present and future sigma levels, process capabilities?
<--- Score

55. How do controls support value?
<--- Score

56. Are you measuring, monitoring and predicting Business Model Innovation activities to optimize operations and profitability, and enhancing outcomes?
<--- Score

57. Is there a recommended audit plan for routine surveillance inspections of Business Model Innovation's gains?
<--- Score

58. How will the day-to-day responsibilities for monitoring and continual improvement be

transferred from the improvement team to the process owner?
<--- Score

59. How will you measure your QA plan's effectiveness?
<--- Score

60. What should you measure to verify efficiency gains?
<--- Score

61. What are customers monitoring?
<--- Score

62. How will input, process, and output variables be checked to detect for sub-optimal conditions?
<--- Score

63. What quality tools were useful in the control phase?
<--- Score

64. Will the team be available to assist members in planning investigations?
<--- Score

65. Has the improved process and its steps been standardized?
<--- Score

66. How do your controls stack up?
<--- Score

67. How do you encourage people to take control and responsibility?

<--- Score

68. How do you monitor usage and cost?
<--- Score

69. How is change control managed?
<--- Score

70. Is a response plan in place for when the input, process, or output measures indicate an 'out-of-control' condition?
<--- Score

71. Is there a documented and implemented monitoring plan?
<--- Score

72. Does Business Model Innovation appropriately measure and monitor risk?
<--- Score

73. What other systems, operations, processes, and infrastructures (hiring practices, staffing, training, incentives/rewards, metrics/dashboards/scorecards, etc.) need updates, additions, changes, or deletions in order to facilitate knowledge transfer and improvements?
<--- Score

74. Is reporting being used or needed?
<--- Score

75. In the case of a Business Model Innovation project, the criteria for the audit derive from implementation objectives, an audit of a Business Model Innovation project involves assessing whether

the recommendations outlined for implementation have been met, can you track that any Business Model Innovation project is implemented as planned, and is it working?
<--- Score

76. Who will be in control?
<--- Score

77. What are the key elements of your Business Model Innovation performance improvement system, including your evaluation, organizational learning, and innovation processes?
<--- Score

78. Do you monitor the effectiveness of your Business Model Innovation activities?
<--- Score

79. How do you spread information?
<--- Score

80. Is there a standardized process?
<--- Score

81. What are your results for key measures or indicators of the accomplishment of your Business Model Innovation strategy and action plans, including building and strengthening core competencies?
<--- Score

82. How will new or emerging customer needs/requirements be checked/communicated to orient the process toward meeting the new specifications and continually reducing variation?
<--- Score

83. Does the response plan contain a definite closed loop continual improvement scheme (e.g., plan-do-check-act)?
<--- Score

84. How do you establish and deploy modified action plans if circumstances require a shift in plans and rapid execution of new plans?
<--- Score

85. Where do ideas that reach policy makers and planners as proposals for Business Model Innovation strengthening and reform actually originate?
<--- Score

86. How likely is the current Business Model Innovation plan to come in on schedule or on budget?
<--- Score

87. Are the planned controls in place?
<--- Score

88. What are the critical parameters to watch?
<--- Score

89. What is the control/monitoring plan?
<--- Score

90. Against what alternative is success being measured?
<--- Score

91. Implementation Planning: is a pilot needed to test the changes before a full roll out occurs?

<--- Score

92. Are pertinent alerts monitored, analyzed and distributed to appropriate personnel?
<--- Score

93. Will your goals reflect your program budget?
<--- Score

94. How do you plan on providing proper recognition and disclosure of supporting companies?
<--- Score

95. Who is the Business Model Innovation process owner?
<--- Score

Add up total points for this section:
_ _ _ _ _ = Total points for this section

Divided by: _ _ _ _ _ _ (number of statements answered) = _ _ _ _ _ _
Average score for this section

Transfer your score to the Business Model Innovation Index at the beginning of the Self-Assessment.

CRITERION #7: SUSTAIN:

INTENT: Retain the benefits.

In my belief, the answer to this question is clearly defined:

5 Strongly Agree

4 Agree

3 Neutral

2 Disagree

1 Strongly Disagree

1. How do you govern and fulfill your societal responsibilities?
<--- Score

2. Who, on the executive team or the board, has spoken to a customer recently?
<--- Score

3. Which individuals, teams or departments will be involved in Business Model Innovation?
<--- Score

4. What happens at your organization when people fail?
<--- Score

5. Do you know what you are doing? And who do you call if you don't?
<--- Score

6. Has the provider been able to innovate with new business models and new sources of revenue?
<--- Score

7. How much does Business Model Innovation help?
<--- Score

8. Do you say no to customers for no reason?
<--- Score

9. Which models, tools and techniques are necessary?
<--- Score

10. Are the assumptions believable and achievable?
<--- Score

11. Were lessons learned captured and communicated?
<--- Score

12. Have benefits been optimized with all key stakeholders?
<--- Score

13. To whom do you add value?
<--- Score

14. What is the recommended frequency of auditing?
<--- Score

15. How can your Procure-to-pay explore business model innovation?
<--- Score

16. What threat is Business Model Innovation addressing?
<--- Score

17. Will there be any necessary staff changes (redundancies or new hires)?
<--- Score

18. What are your most important goals for the strategic Business Model Innovation objectives?
<--- Score

19. How do you lead with Business Model Innovation in mind?
<--- Score

20. What counts that you are not counting?
<--- Score

21. Operational - will it work?
<--- Score

22. How do senior leaders deploy your organizations vision and values through your leadership system, to the workforce, to key suppliers and partners, and to customers and other stakeholders, as appropriate?
<--- Score

23. How can you become more high-tech but still be

high touch?

<--- Score

24. Is there any existing Business Model Innovation governance structure?

<--- Score

25. What must you excel at?

<--- Score

26. How do you explore business model innovation?

<--- Score

27. What are you challenging?

<--- Score

28. What could happen if you do not do it?

<--- Score

29. What are internal and external Business Model Innovation relations?

<--- Score

30. How long will it take to change?

<--- Score

31. What is your competitive advantage?

<--- Score

32. Why will customers want to buy your organizations products/services?

<--- Score

33. What is the source of the strategies for Business Model Innovation strengthening and reform?

<--- Score

34. What is a feasible sequencing of reform initiatives over time?
<--- Score

35. Instead of going to current contacts for new ideas, what if you reconnected with dormant contacts-- the people you used to know? If you were going reactivate a dormant tie, who would it be?
<--- Score

36. What happens if you do not have enough funding?
<--- Score

37. What are specific Business Model Innovation rules to follow?
<--- Score

38. Are you making progress, and are you making progress as Business Model Innovation leaders?
<--- Score

39. Who will provide the final approval of Business Model Innovation deliverables?
<--- Score

40. What is your BATNA (best alternative to a negotiated agreement)?
<--- Score

41. Who are the key stakeholders?
<--- Score

42. Are you maintaining a past–present–future

perspective throughout the Business Model Innovation discussion?

<--- Score

43. What was the last experiment you ran?

<--- Score

44. What is the big Business Model Innovation idea?

<--- Score

45. How can you become the company that would put you out of business?

<--- Score

46. What relationships among Business Model Innovation trends do you perceive?

<--- Score

47. How do you create buy-in?

<--- Score

48. Is a Business Model Innovation team work effort in place?

<--- Score

49. How will you insure seamless interoperability of Business Model Innovation moving forward?

<--- Score

50. How do you foster innovation?

<--- Score

51. Why is Business Model Innovation important for you now?

<--- Score

52. What business benefits will Business Model Innovation goals deliver if achieved?
<--- Score

53. Which Business Model Innovation goals are the most important?
<--- Score

54. What does your signature ensure?
<--- Score

55. What management system can you use to leverage the Business Model Innovation experience, ideas, and concerns of the people closest to the work to be done?
<--- Score

56. What is the funding source for this project?
<--- Score

57. Who will manage the integration of tools?
<--- Score

58. What is the kind of project structure that would be appropriate for your Business Model Innovation project, should it be formal and complex, or can it be less formal and relatively simple?
<--- Score

59. What is the business model innovation?
<--- Score

60. How will you ensure you get what you expected?
<--- Score

61. Can you do all this work?

<--- Score

62. What knowledge, skills and characteristics mark a good Business Model Innovation project manager?
<--- Score

63. What are the barriers to increased Business Model Innovation production?
<--- Score

64. What Business Model Innovation skills are most important?
<--- Score

65. Are all key stakeholders present at all Structured Walkthroughs?
<--- Score

66. How much contingency will be available in the budget?
<--- Score

67. How do you know if you are successful?
<--- Score

68. How do you stay inspired?
<--- Score

69. What goals did you miss?
<--- Score

70. What would have to be true for the option on the table to be the best possible choice?
<--- Score

71. Do you think Business Model Innovation

accomplishes the goals you expect it to accomplish?
<--- Score

72. Who are your customers?
<--- Score

73. Is the impact that Business Model Innovation has shown?
<--- Score

74. How do you determine the key elements that affect Business Model Innovation workforce satisfaction, how are these elements determined for different workforce groups and segments?
<--- Score

75. Are new benefits received and understood?
<--- Score

76. Who else should you help?
<--- Score

77. Are you relevant? Will you be relevant five years from now? Ten?
<--- Score

78. Which functions and people interact with the supplier and or customer?
<--- Score

79. Who do you want your customers to become?
<--- Score

80. If you were responsible for initiating and implementing major changes in your organization, what steps might you take to ensure acceptance of

those changes?
<--- Score

81. What one word do you want to own in the minds of your customers, employees, and partners?
<--- Score

82. In retrospect, of the projects that you pulled the plug on, what percent do you wish had been allowed to keep going, and what percent do you wish had ended earlier?
<--- Score

83. Who have you, as a company, historically been when you've been at your best?
<--- Score

84. What will be the consequences to the stakeholder (financial, reputation etc) if Business Model Innovation does not go ahead or fails to deliver the objectives?
<--- Score

85. What potential megatrends could make your business model obsolete?
<--- Score

86. Would you rather sell to knowledgeable and informed customers or to uninformed customers?
<--- Score

87. What is your Business Model Innovation strategy?
<--- Score

88. Do you have an implicit bias for capital investments over people investments?
<--- Score

89. Who is responsible for errors?
<--- Score

90. What is the purpose of Business Model Innovation in relation to the mission?
<--- Score

91. What are the short and long-term Business Model Innovation goals?
<--- Score

92. What is the overall talent health of your organization as a whole at senior levels, and for each organization reporting to a member of the Senior Leadership Team?
<--- Score

93. What are the usability implications of Business Model Innovation actions?
<--- Score

94. What is your question? Why?
<--- Score

95. What have you done to protect your business from competitive encroachment?
<--- Score

96. Do you feel that more should be done in the Business Model Innovation area?
<--- Score

97. Who do we want your customers to become?
<--- Score

98. How do you ensure that implementations of Business Model Innovation products are done in a way that ensures safety?
<--- Score

99. If you weren't already in this business, would you enter it today? And if not, what are you going to do about it?
<--- Score

100. If your company went out of business tomorrow, would anyone who doesn't get a paycheck here care?
<--- Score

101. Political -is anyone trying to undermine this project?
<--- Score

102. How do you accomplish your long range Business Model Innovation goals?
<--- Score

103. Are you / should you be revolutionary or evolutionary?
<--- Score

104. What is the craziest thing you can do?
<--- Score

105. Who will determine interim and final deadlines?
<--- Score

106. How will you motivate the stakeholders with the least vested interest?
<--- Score

107. How do you provide a safe environment
-physically and emotionally?
<--- Score

108. Why not do Business Model Innovation?
<--- Score

109. Think of your Business Model Innovation project,
what are the main functions?
<--- Score

110. Why do and why don't your customers like your
organization?
<--- Score

111. How do you keep records, of what?
<--- Score

112. Are you satisfied with your current role? If not,
what is missing from it?
<--- Score

113. How likely is it that a customer would
recommend your company to a friend or colleague?
<--- Score

114. What have been your experiences in defining
long range Business Model Innovation goals?
<--- Score

115. What information is critical to your organization
that your executives are ignoring?
<--- Score

116. Is there a work around that you can use?
<--- Score

117. How do you maintain Business Model Innovation's Integrity?
<--- Score

118. How do you deal with Business Model Innovation changes?
<--- Score

119. Who uses your product in ways you never expected?
<--- Score

120. What is your formula for success in Business Model Innovation ?
<--- Score

121. In the past year, what have you done (or could you have done) to increase the accurate perception of your company/brand as ethical and honest?
<--- Score

122. How important is Business Model Innovation to the user organizations mission?
<--- Score

123. What do we do when new problems arise?
<--- Score

124. Who is on the team?
<--- Score

125. Who is responsible for Business Model Innovation?
<--- Score

126. What are your personal philosophies regarding Business Model Innovation and how do they influence your work?
<--- Score

127. What are the rules and assumptions your industry operates under? What if the opposite were true?
<--- Score

128. How do customers see your organization?
<--- Score

129. Is Business Model Innovation dependent on the successful delivery of a current project?
<--- Score

130. If your customer were your grandmother, would you tell her to buy what you're selling?
<--- Score

131. What Business Model Innovation modifications can you make work for you?
<--- Score

132. What are you trying to prove to yourself, and how might it be hijacking your life and business success?
<--- Score

133. How is implementation research currently incorporated into each of your goals?
<--- Score

134. What are the business goals Business Model Innovation is aiming to achieve?
<--- Score

135. How do you assess the Business Model Innovation pitfalls that are inherent in implementing it?

<--- Score

136. What may be the consequences for the performance of an organization if all stakeholders are not consulted regarding Business Model Innovation?

<--- Score

137. Are you paying enough attention to the partners your company depends on to succeed?

<--- Score

138. What is your objective for business model innovation?

<--- Score

139. What projects are going on in the organization today, and what resources are those projects using from the resource pools?

<--- Score

140. What is the range of capabilities?

<--- Score

141. How does Business Model Innovation integrate with other stakeholder initiatives?

<--- Score

142. Is it economical; do you have the time and money?

<--- Score

143. What are you doing in your business model innovation based on or adding sustainability?

<--- Score

144. Is a Business Model Innovation breakthrough on the horizon?
<--- Score

145. If you do not follow, then how to lead?
<--- Score

146. How do you engage the workforce, in addition to satisfying them?
<--- Score

147. Are assumptions made in Business Model Innovation stated explicitly?
<--- Score

148. How do you make it meaningful in connecting Business Model Innovation with what users do day-to-day?
<--- Score

149. Whom among your colleagues do you trust, and for what?
<--- Score

150. What unique value proposition (UVP) do you offer?
<--- Score

151. Is the Business Model Innovation organization completing tasks effectively and efficiently?
<--- Score

152. What trouble can you get into?
<--- Score

153. Why should you adopt a Business Model Innovation framework?
<--- Score

154. What is something you believe that nearly no one agrees with you on?
<--- Score

155. Is there any reason to believe the opposite of my current belief?
<--- Score

156. What are strategies for increasing support and reducing opposition?
<--- Score

157. When information truly is ubiquitous, when reach and connectivity are completely global, when computing resources are infinite, and when a whole new set of impossibilities are not only possible, but happening, what will that do to your business?
<--- Score

158. What you are going to do to affect the numbers?
<--- Score

159. Do you think you know, or do you know you know ?
<--- Score

160. Do you see more potential in people than they do in themselves?
<--- Score

161. What are the potential basics of Business Model

Innovation fraud?
<--- Score

162. What is the overall business strategy?
<--- Score

163. What are the top 3 things at the forefront of your Business Model Innovation agendas for the next 3 years?
<--- Score

164. Who do you think the world wants your organization to be?
<--- Score

165. How can you incorporate support to ensure safe and effective use of Business Model Innovation into the services that you provide?
<--- Score

166. Do you have the right people on the bus?
<--- Score

167. Whose voice (department, ethnic group, women, older workers, etc) might you have missed hearing from in your company, and how might you amplify this voice to create positive momentum for your business?
<--- Score

168. Do you have the right capabilities and capacities?
<--- Score

169. What are the success criteria that will indicate that Business Model Innovation objectives have been met and the benefits delivered?

<--- Score

170. Is Business Model Innovation realistic, or are you setting yourself up for failure?
<--- Score

171. What is the effect of Digital Twins on service business model innovation?
<--- Score

172. How do you go about securing Business Model Innovation?
<--- Score

173. How do you listen to customers to obtain actionable information?
<--- Score

174. At what moment would you think; Will I get fired?
<--- Score

175. What role does communication play in the success or failure of a Business Model Innovation project?
<--- Score

176. Have new benefits been realized?
<--- Score

177. Where can you break convention?
<--- Score

178. Do you know who is a friend or a foe?
<--- Score

179. Is your strategy driving your strategy? Or is the

way in which you allocate resources driving your strategy?

<--- Score

180. Are there any activities that you can take off your to do list?

<--- Score

181. Who is the main stakeholder, with ultimate responsibility for driving Business Model Innovation forward?

<--- Score

182. Are the criteria for selecting recommendations stated?

<--- Score

183. Ask yourself: how would you do this work if you only had one staff member to do it?

<--- Score

184. How can your organization explore business model innovation?

<--- Score

185. Are you changing as fast as the world around you?

<--- Score

186. Do you have enough freaky customers in your portfolio pushing you to the limit day in and day out?

<--- Score

187. Did your employees make progress today?

<--- Score

188. How do you track customer value, profitability or financial return, organizational success, and sustainability?
<--- Score

189. Who are four people whose careers you have enhanced?
<--- Score

190. What is it like to work for you?
<--- Score

191. Who is responsible for ensuring appropriate resources (time, people and money) are allocated to Business Model Innovation?
<--- Score

192. Can the schedule be done in the given time?
<--- Score

193. Is maximizing Business Model Innovation protection the same as minimizing Business Model Innovation loss?
<--- Score

194. How does your BizOps explore business model innovation?
<--- Score

195. How do you keep the momentum going?
<--- Score

196. What are the challenges?
<--- Score

197. If you had to leave your organization for a year

and the only communication you could have with employees/colleagues was a single paragraph, what would you write?
<--- Score

198. Do you have past Business Model Innovation successes?
<--- Score

199. Are your responses positive or negative?
<--- Score

200. What are the long-term Business Model Innovation goals?
<--- Score

201. How do you foster the skills, knowledge, talents, attributes, and characteristics you want to have?
<--- Score

202. What should you stop doing?
<--- Score

203. What did you miss in the interview for the worst hire you ever made?
<--- Score

204. Will it be accepted by users?
<--- Score

205. Do Business Model Innovation rules make a reasonable demand on a users capabilities?
<--- Score

206. Who will be responsible for deciding whether Business Model Innovation goes ahead or not after

the initial investigations?
<--- Score

207. What is your business model innovation?
<--- Score

208. What stupid rule would you most like to kill?
<--- Score

209. Can you maintain your growth without detracting from the factors that have contributed to your success?
<--- Score

210. What trophy do you want on your mantle?
<--- Score

211. If no one would ever find out about your accomplishments, how would you lead differently?
<--- Score

212. How does your organization explore business model innovation?
<--- Score

213. How do you manage Business Model Innovation Knowledge Management (KM)?
<--- Score

214. What is an unauthorized commitment?
<--- Score

215. Has implementation been effective in reaching specified objectives so far?
<--- Score

216. What is effective Business Model Innovation?
<--- Score

217. Why should people listen to you?
<--- Score

218. Why is it important to have senior management support for a Business Model Innovation project?
<--- Score

Add up total points for this section:
_____ = Total points for this section

Divided by: _____ (number of statements answered) = _____
Average score for this section

Transfer your score to the Business Model Innovation Index at the beginning of the Self-Assessment.

Business Model Innovation and Managing Projects, Criteria for Project Managers:

1.0 Initiating Process Group: Business Model Innovation

1. What will you do?

2. How well did the chosen processes produce the expected results?

3. Do you know the roles & responsibilities required for this Business Model Innovation project?

4. What do they need to know about the Business Model Innovation project?

5. Realistic - are the desired results expressed in a way that the team will be motivated and believe that the required level of involvement will be obtained?

6. When are the deliverables to be generated in each phase?

7. What are the constraints?

8. What will you do to minimize the impact should a risk event occur?

9. Were decisions made in a timely manner?

10. Are stakeholders properly informed about the status of the Business Model Innovation project?

11. Are there resources to maintain and support the outcome of the Business Model Innovation project?

12. What are the pressing issues of the hour?

13. Who are the Business Model Innovation project stakeholders?

14. What must be done?

15. At which cmmi level are software processes documented, standardized, and integrated into a standard to-be practiced process for your organization?

16. What technical work to do in each phase?

17. If action is called for, what form should it take?

18. Based on your Business Model Innovation project communication management plan, what worked well?

19. Do you understand all business (operational), technical, resource and vendor risks associated with the Business Model Innovation project?

1.1 Project Charter: Business Model Innovation

20. When do you use a Business Model Innovation project Charter?

21. Why the improvements?

22. If finished, on what date did it finish?

23. Name and describe the elements that deal with providing the detail?

24. Major high-level milestone targets: what events measure progress?

25. What are you trying to accomplish?

26. How will you know that a change is an improvement?

27. Who will take notes, document decisions?

28. How high should you set your goals?

29. What goes into your Business Model Innovation project Charter?

30. What is the most common tool for helping define the detail?

31. How are Business Model Innovation projects different from operations?

32. Business Model Innovation project objective statement: what must the Business Model Innovation project do?

33. What is the purpose of the Business Model Innovation project?

34. Success determination factors: how will the success of the Business Model Innovation project be determined from the customers perspective?

35. Who manages integration?

36. Who ise input and support will this Business Model Innovation project require?

37. Why use a Business Model Innovation project charter?

38. What outcome, in measureable terms, are you hoping to accomplish?

1.2 Stakeholder Register: Business Model Innovation

39. How should employers make voices heard?

40. Who are the stakeholders?

41. What are the major Business Model Innovation project milestones requiring communications or providing communications opportunities?

42. Who is managing stakeholder engagement?

43. What opportunities exist to provide communications?

44. What & Why?

45. What is the power of the stakeholder?

46. Who wants to talk about Security?

47. Is your organization ready for change?

48. How will reports be created?

49. How big is the gap?

50. How much influence do they have on the Business Model Innovation project?

1.3 Stakeholder Analysis Matrix: Business Model Innovation

51. Do the stakeholders goals and expectations support or conflict with the Business Model Innovation project goals?

52. Who will be affected by the Business Model Innovation project?

53. It developments?

54. What can the stakeholder prevent from happening?

55. What could your organization improve?

56. Lack of competitive strength?

57. Accreditations, qualifications, certifications?

58. How to measure the achievement of the Development Objective?

59. Benefit to whom?

60. What is accountability in relation to the Business Model Innovation project?

61. Who are potential allies and opponents?

62. Why do you care?

63. How do rules, behaviors affect stakes?

64. What are the opportunities for communication?

65. Resource providers; who can provide resources to ensure the implementation of the Business Model Innovation project?

66. How can you counter negative efforts?

67. What is your Advocacy Strategy?

68. What obstacles does your organization face?

69. Resources, assets, people?

2.0 Planning Process Group: Business Model Innovation

70. Have operating capacities been created and/or reinforced in partners?

71. If task x starts two days late, what is the effect on the Business Model Innovation project end date?

72. What factors are contributing to progress or delay in the achievement of products and results?

73. Will you be replaced?

74. If a risk event occurs, what will you do?

75. What is the difference between the early schedule and late schedule?

76. What do you need to do?

77. How does activity resource estimation affect activity duration estimation?

78. To what extent have the target population and participants made the activities own, taking an active role in it?

79. Business Model Innovation project assessment; why did you do this Business Model Innovation project?

80. Is the identification of the problems, inequalities

and gaps, with respective causes, clear in the Business Model Innovation project?

81. To what extent has the intervention strategy been adapted to the areas of intervention in which it is being implemented?

82. What should you do next?

83. Product breakdown structure (pbs): what is the Business Model Innovation project result or product, and how should it look like, what are its parts?

84. Who are the Business Model Innovation project stakeholders?

85. What types of differentiated effects are resulting from the Business Model Innovation project and to what extent?

86. How can you tell when you are done?

87. Contingency planning. if a risk event occurs, what will you do?

88. Are the follow-up indicators relevant and do they meet the quality needed to measure the outputs and outcomes of the Business Model Innovation project?

2.1 Project Management Plan: Business Model Innovation

89. Does the selected plan protect privacy?

90. What are the assigned resources?

91. Who is the Business Model Innovation project Manager?

92. What is Business Model Innovation project scope management?

93. Was the peer (technical) review of the cost estimates duly coordinated with the cost estimate center of expertise and addressed in the review documentation and certification?

94. Is mitigation authorized or recommended?

95. Are alternatives safe, functional, constructible, economical, reasonable and sustainable?

96. Where does all this information come from?

97. What would you do differently?

98. What are the assumptions?

99. Is the budget realistic?

100. Is there anything you would now do differently on your Business Model Innovation project based on

past experience?

101. Has the selected plan been formulated using cost effectiveness and incremental analysis techniques?

102. Will you add a schedule and diagram?

103. If the Business Model Innovation project management plan is a comprehensive document that guides you in Business Model Innovation project execution and control, then what should it NOT contain?

104. Are there non-structural buyout or relocation recommendations?

105. Are there any scope changes proposed for a previously authorized Business Model Innovation project?

106. What if, for example, the positive direction and vision of your organization causes expected trends to change resulting in greater need than expected?

107. Are cost risk analysis methods applied to develop contingencies for the estimated total Business Model Innovation project costs?

108. What should you drop in order to add something new?

2.2 Scope Management Plan: Business Model Innovation

109. Timeline and milestones?

110. What weaknesses do you have?

111. Have the personnel with the necessary skills and competence been identified and has agreement for participation in the Business Model Innovation project been reached with the appropriate management?

112. Are adequate resources provided for the quality assurance function?

113. Are meeting minutes captured and sent out after the meeting?

114. Have Business Model Innovation project team accountabilities & responsibilities been clearly defined?

115. What are the acceptance criteria (process and criteria to be met for key stakeholder acceptance) and who is authorized to sign off?

116. Do you document disagreements and work towards resolutions?

117. Does the Business Model Innovation project team have the skills necessary to successfully complete current Business Model Innovation project(s) and support the application?

118. Is there a formal set of procedures supporting Stakeholder Management?

119. Have Business Model Innovation project success criteria been defined?

120. Has the schedule been baselined?

121. Assess the expected stability of the scope of this Business Model Innovation project how likely is it to change, how frequently, and by how much?

122. Have you identified possible roadblocks?

123. Is your organization structure for both tracking & controlling the budget well defined and assigned to a specific individual?

124. Are all resource assumptions documented?

125. Are you spending the right amount of money for specific tasks?

126. Are internal Business Model Innovation project status meetings held at reasonable intervals?

127. Has the Business Model Innovation project manager been identified?

2.3 Requirements Management Plan: Business Model Innovation

128. Is the user satisfied?

129. Do you have an appropriate arrangement for meetings?

130. How will bidders price evaluations be done, by deliverables, phases, or in a big bang?

131. Is the change control process documented?

132. What is a problem?

133. Do you know which stakeholders will participate in the requirements effort?

134. Who is responsible for quantifying the Business Model Innovation project requirements?

135. Did you avoid subjective, flowery or non-specific statements?

136. How will you communicate scheduled tasks to other team members?

137. Is any organizational data being used or stored?

138. How will the information be distributed?

139. Who will approve the requirements (and if multiple approvers, in what order)?

140. Will the Business Model Innovation project requirements become approved in writing?

141. How often will the reporting occur?

142. What information regarding the Business Model Innovation project requirements will be reported?

143. What are you trying to do?

144. Do you have price sheets and a methodology for determining the total proposal cost?

145. What performance metrics will be used?

146. Will you use an assessment of the Business Model Innovation project environment as a tool to discover risk to the requirements process?

147. Who has the authority to reject Business Model Innovation project requirements?

2.4 Requirements Documentation: Business Model Innovation

148. How do you get the user to tell you what they want?

149. What kind of entity is a problem ?

150. Consistency. are there any requirements conflicts?

151. Where do system and software requirements come from, what are sources?

152. Can the requirement be changed without a large impact on other requirements?

153. Does your organization restrict technical alternatives?

154. Who provides requirements?

155. Is the origin of the requirement clearly stated?

156. What variations exist for a process?

157. Where do you define what is a customer, what are the attributes of customer?

158. The problem with gathering requirements is right there in the word gathering. What images does it conjure?

159. Where are business rules being captured?

160. What is the risk associated with cost and schedule?

161. How will requirements be documented and who signs off on them?

162. Who is involved?

163. Verifiability. can the requirements be checked?

164. What marketing channels do you want to use: e-mail, letter or sms?

165. Do technical resources exist?

166. What is a show stopper in the requirements?

167. How will the proposed Business Model Innovation project help?

2.5 Requirements Traceability Matrix: Business Model Innovation

168. Will you use a Requirements Traceability Matrix?

169. Why use a WBS?

170. How will it affect the stakeholders personally in career?

171. Describe the process for approving requirements so they can be added to the traceability matrix and Business Model Innovation project work can be performed. Will the Business Model Innovation project requirements become approved in writing?

172. How small is small enough?

173. Why do you manage scope?

174. Is there a requirements traceability process in place?

175. Do you have a clear understanding of all subcontracts in place?

176. How do you manage scope?

177. What are the chronologies, contingencies, consequences, criteria?

178. What percentage of Business Model Innovation projects are producing traceability matrices between

requirements and other work products?

179. What is the WBS?

2.6 Project Scope Statement: Business Model Innovation

180. Relevant - ask yourself can you get there; why are you doing this Business Model Innovation project?

181. Is the change control process documented and on file?

182. Is there a process (test plans, inspections, reviews) defined for verifying outputs for each task?

183. Write a brief purpose statement for this Business Model Innovation project. Include a business justification statement. What is the product of this Business Model Innovation project?

184. Is there a baseline plan against which to measure progress?

185. How often will scope changes be reviewed?

186. Were key Business Model Innovation project stakeholders brought into the Business Model Innovation project Plan?

187. Is the plan under configuration management?

188. Will this process be communicated to the customer and Business Model Innovation project team?

189. Business Model Innovation project lead, team

lead, solution architect?

190. Has everyone approved the Business Model Innovation projects scope statement?

191. Is an issue management process documented and filed?

192. If there are vendors, have they signed off on the Business Model Innovation project Plan?

193. Is the quality function identified and assigned?

194. What actions will be taken to mitigate the risk?

195. Is the Business Model Innovation project manager qualified and experienced in Business Model Innovation project management?

196. Have the configuration management functions been assigned?

197. Will you need a statement of work?

2.7 Assumption and Constraint Log: Business Model Innovation

198. What worked well?

199. Would known impacts serve as impediments?

200. Have you eliminated all duplicative tasks or manual efforts, where appropriate?

201. If it is out of compliance, should the process be amended or should the Plan be amended?

202. Is there adequate stakeholder participation for the vetting of requirements definition, changes and management?

203. Have all stakeholders been identified?

204. Does the plan conform to standards?

205. Is the amount of effort justified by the anticipated value of forming a new process?

206. Has a Business Model Innovation project Communications Plan been developed?

207. Have all involved stakeholders and work groups committed to the Business Model Innovation project?

208. Is the steering committee active in Business Model Innovation project oversight?

209. Is there documentation of system capability requirements, data requirements, environment requirements, security requirements, and computer and hardware requirements?

210. Do the requirements meet the standards of correctness, completeness, consistency, accuracy, and readability?

211. Should factors be unpredictable over time?

212. How are new requirements or changes to requirements identified?

213. Is this process still needed?

214. No superfluous information or marketing narrative?

215. Are there nonconformance issues?

216. Have the scope, objectives, costs, benefits and impacts been communicated to all involved and/or impacted stakeholders and work groups?

217. Is the current scope of the Business Model Innovation project substantially different than that originally defined in the approved Business Model Innovation project plan?

2.8 Work Breakdown Structure: Business Model Innovation

218. Is the work breakdown structure (wbs) defined and is the scope of the Business Model Innovation project clear with assigned deliverable owners?

219. Is it still viable?

220. Where does it take place?

221. When does it have to be done?

222. Is it a change in scope?

223. Why would you develop a Work Breakdown Structure?

224. How far down?

225. How will you and your Business Model Innovation project team define the Business Model Innovation projects scope and work breakdown structure?

226. How big is a work-package?

227. When do you stop?

228. Why is it useful?

229. When would you develop a Work Breakdown Structure?

230. Can you make it?

231. What is the probability of completing the Business Model Innovation project in less that xx days?

232. Who has to do it?

233. What has to be done?

234. Do you need another level?

2.9 WBS Dictionary: Business Model Innovation

235. Are indirect costs charged to the appropriate indirect pools and incurring organization?

236. Where learning is used in developing underlying budgets is there a direct relationship between anticipated learning and time phased budgets?

237. Is the work done on a work package level as described in the WBS dictionary?

238. Changes in the direct base to which overhead costs are allocated?

239. Is work properly classified as measured effort, LOE, or apportioned effort and appropriately separated?

240. Are data elements (BCWS, BCWP, and ACWP) progressively summarized from the detail level to the contract level through the CWBS?

241. Are overhead cost budgets (or Business Model Innovation projections) established on a facility-wide basis at least annually for the life of the contract?

242. Are work packages reasonably short in time duration or do they have adequate objective indicators/milestones to minimize subjectivity of the in process work evaluation?

243. Are data elements summarized through the functional organizational structure for progressively higher levels of management?

244. Changes in the nature of the overhead requirements?

245. Is all budget available as management reserve identified and excluded from the performance measurement baseline?

246. Wbs elements contractually specified for reporting of status to you (lowest level only)?

247. Are the procedures for identifying indirect costs to incurring organizations, indirect cost pools, and allocating the costs from the pools to the contracts formally documented?

248. Are overhead cost budgets established for each organization which has authority to incur overhead costs?

249. The already stated responsible for overhead performance control of related costs?

250. Are indirect costs accumulated for comparison with the corresponding budgets?

251. Are the overhead pools formally and adequately identified?

252. Does the contractors system description or procedures require that the performance measurement baseline plus management reserve equal the contract budget base?

253. Are the requirements for all items of overhead established by rational, traceable processes?

254. Are retroactive changes to direct costs and indirect costs prohibited except for the correction of errors and routine accounting adjustments?

2.10 Schedule Management Plan: Business Model Innovation

255. Are all vendor contracts closed out?

256. Does the ims reflect accurate current status and credible start/finish forecasts for all to-go tasks and milestones?

257. Does the ims include all contract and/or designated management control milestones?

258. Are cause and effect determined for risks when they occur?

259. Are the Business Model Innovation project team members located locally to the users/stakeholders?

260. Are Business Model Innovation project team members committed fulltime?

261. Have all team members been part of identifying risks?

262. How are Business Model Innovation projects different from operations?

263. Business Model Innovation project definition & scope?

264. Is the steering committee active in Business Model Innovation project oversight?

265. Are the predecessor and successor relationships accurate?

266. Has a quality assurance plan been developed for the Business Model Innovation project?

267. Why conduct schedule analysis?

268. Are actuals compared against estimates to analyze and correct variances?

269. Can additional resources be added to subsequent tasks to reduce the durations of the already stated tasks?

270. Was your organizations estimating methodology being used and followed?

271. Has the scope management document been updated and distributed to help prevent scope creep?

272. Are there any activities or deliverables being added or gold-plated that could be dropped or scaled back without falling short of the original requirement?

273. Is pert / critical path or equivalent methodology being used?

2.11 Activity List: Business Model Innovation

274. What are you counting on?

275. When will the work be performed?

276. Is there anything planned that does not need to be here?

277. What did not go as well?

278. Where will it be performed?

279. What is your organizations history in doing similar activities?

280. Can you determine the activity that must finish, before this activity can start?

281. For other activities, how much delay can be tolerated?

282. How should ongoing costs be monitored to try to keep the Business Model Innovation project within budget?

283. How difficult will it be to do specific activities on this Business Model Innovation project?

284. What went right?

285. What is the LF and LS for each activity?

286. Is infrastructure setup part of your Business Model Innovation project?

287. What will be performed?

288. The wbs is developed as part of a joint planning session. and how do you know that youhave done this right?

289. What is the probability the Business Model Innovation project can be completed in xx weeks?

290. What is the total time required to complete the Business Model Innovation project if no delays occur?

291. How detailed should a Business Model Innovation project get?

292. What went well?

293. What are the critical bottleneck activities?

2.12 Activity Attributes: Business Model Innovation

294. Has management defined a definite timeframe for the turnaround or Business Model Innovation project window?

295. Do you feel very comfortable with your prediction?

296. Activity: what is Missing?

297. Are the required resources available or need to be acquired?

298. How many days do you need to complete the work scope with a limit of X number of resources?

299. Where else does it apply?

300. How much activity detail is required?

301. Were there other ways you could have organized the data to achieve similar results?

302. What is the general pattern here?

303. Have you identified the Activity Leveling Priority code value on each activity?

304. Activity: what is In the Bag?

305. Does your organization of the data change its

meaning?

306. What activity do you think you should spend the most time on?

307. Have constraints been applied to the start and finish milestones for the phases?

308. What went wrong?

309. Are the required resources available?

310. What is missing?

311. Would you consider either of corresponding activities an outlier?

2.13 Milestone List: Business Model Innovation

312. Insurmountable weaknesses?

313. Sustaining internal capabilities?

314. Obstacles faced?

315. Continuity, supply chain robustness?

316. What is the market for your technology, product or service?

317. What has been done so far?

318. How late can the activity start?

319. Gaps in capabilities?

320. What specific improvements did you make to the Business Model Innovation project proposal since the previous time?

321. Reliability of data, plan predictability?

322. Level of the Innovation?

323. Vital contracts and partners?

324. What background experience, skills, and strengths does the team bring to your organization?

325. Environmental effects?

326. Political effects?

327. Marketing - reach, distribution, awareness?

328. It is to be a narrative text providing the crucial aspects of your Business Model Innovation project proposal answering what, who, how, when and where?

329. How do you manage time?

2.14 Network Diagram: Business Model Innovation

330. What job or jobs follow it?

331. How difficult will it be to do specific activities on this Business Model Innovation project?

332. How confident can you be in your milestone dates and the delivery date?

333. If x is long, what would be the completion time if you break x into two parallel parts of y weeks and z weeks?

334. What are the Key Success Factors?

335. What can be done concurrently?

336. What job or jobs precede it?

337. What to do and When?

338. What is the probability of completing the Business Model Innovation project in less that xx days?

339. What controls the start and finish of a job?

340. If the Business Model Innovation project network diagram cannot change and you have extra personnel resources, what is the BEST thing to do?

341. What is the completion time?

342. What activities must occur simultaneously with this activity?

343. Where do schedules come from?

344. What are the tools?

345. Planning: who, how long, what to do?

346. Why must you schedule milestones, such as reviews, throughout the Business Model Innovation project?

347. Are you on time?

348. What is the lowest cost to complete this Business Model Innovation project in xx weeks?

2.15 Activity Resource Requirements: Business Model Innovation

349. Are there unresolved issues that need to be addressed?

350. Other support in specific areas?

351. When does monitoring begin?

352. What are constraints that you might find during the Human Resource Planning process?

353. Organizational Applicability?

354. How many signatures do you require on a check and does this match what is in your policy and procedures?

355. Why do you do that?

356. Anything else?

357. Time for overtime?

358. Which logical relationship does the PDM use most often?

359. How do you handle petty cash?

360. What is the Work Plan Standard?

361. Do you use tools like decomposition and rolling-

wave planning to produce the activity list and other outputs?

2.16 Resource Breakdown Structure: Business Model Innovation

362. Who is allowed to see what data about which resources?

363. What is the primary purpose of the human resource plan?

364. How should the information be delivered?

365. Who needs what information?

366. Who will use the system?

367. The list could probably go on, but, the thing that you would most like to know is, How long & How much?

368. What can you do to improve productivity?

369. Changes based on input from stakeholders?

370. Who is allowed to perform which functions?

371. What defines a successful Business Model Innovation project?

372. Why time management?

373. What are the requirements for resource data?

374. What is each stakeholders desired outcome for

the Business Model Innovation project?

375. Which resource planning tool provides information on resource responsibility and accountability?

376. How can this help you with team building?

2.17 Activity Duration Estimates: Business Model Innovation

377. Which best describes how this affects the Business Model Innovation project?

378. What are key inputs and outputs of the software?

379. Do stakeholders follow a procedure for formally accepting the Business Model Innovation project scope?

380. Why is there a new or renewed interest in the field of Business Model Innovation project management?

381. Is the work performed reviewed against contractual objectives?

382. Are team building activities completed to improve team performance?

383. Do you agree with the suggestions provided for improving Business Model Innovation project communications?

384. Are updates on work results collected and used as inputs to the performance reporting process?

385. What are the key components of a Business Model Innovation project communications plan?

386. Are the causes of all variances identified?

387. How many different communications channels does a Business Model Innovation project team with six people have?

388. Which tips for taking the PMP exam do you think would be most helpful for you?

389. On which process should team members spend the most time?

390. What are the main types of goods and services being outsourced?

391. Why is it important to determine activity sequencing on Business Model Innovation projects?

392. What are the typical challenges Business Model Innovation project teams face during each of the five process groups?

393. What tasks must follow this task?

394. Find an example of a contract for information technology services. Analyze the key features of the contract. What type of contract was used and why?

395. Will outside resources be needed to help in its development?

396. What is pmp certification, and why do you think the number of people earning it has grown so much in the past ten years?

2.18 Duration Estimating Worksheet: Business Model Innovation

397. Define the work as completely as possible. What work will be included in the Business Model Innovation project?

398. What is cost and Business Model Innovation project cost management?

399. Do any colleagues have experience with your organization and/or RFPs?

400. What is the total time required to complete the Business Model Innovation project if no delays occur?

401. Does the Business Model Innovation project provide innovative ways for stakeholders to overcome obstacles or deliver better outcomes?

402. When do the individual activities need to start and finish?

403. What work will be included in the Business Model Innovation project?

404. Done before proceeding with this activity or what can be done concurrently?

405. Is the Business Model Innovation project responsive to community need?

406. Why estimate costs?

407. What is an Average Business Model Innovation project?

408. Can the Business Model Innovation project be constructed as planned?

409. When does your organization expect to be able to complete it?

410. What info is needed?

411. Is a construction detail attached (to aid in explanation)?

412. Why estimate time and cost?

2.19 Project Schedule: Business Model Innovation

413. Are activities connected because logic dictates the order in which others occur?

414. Was the Business Model Innovation project schedule reviewed by all stakeholders and formally accepted?

415. How many levels?

416. How much detail?

417. How detailed should a Business Model Innovation project get?

418. Should you have a test for each code module?

419. Did the final product meet or exceed user expectations?

420. What is the most mis-scheduled part of process?

421. Why do you think schedule issues often cause the most conflicts on Business Model Innovation projects?

422. How can you address that situation?

423. How can you shorten the schedule?

424. Why do you need to manage Business Model Innovation project Risk?

425. What documents, if any, will the subcontractor provide (eg Business Model Innovation project schedule, quality plan etc)?

426. Did the Business Model Innovation project come in under budget?

427. Schedule/cost recovery?

428. Are quality inspections and review activities listed in the Business Model Innovation project schedule(s)?

429. How much slack is available in the Business Model Innovation project?

430. What is the purpose of a Business Model Innovation project schedule?

431. Are all remaining durations correct?

432. Should you include sub-activities?

2.20 Cost Management Plan: Business Model Innovation

433. Are milestone deliverables effectively tracked and compared to Business Model Innovation project plan?

434. Technical and functional?

435. For cost control purposes?

436. Is there a formal set of procedures supporting Issues Management?

437. Is your organization certified as a broker of the products/supplies?

438. Contingency – how will cost contingency be administered?

439. Has a sponsor been identified?

440. Owner, contractor, and subcontractors?

441. Are issues raised, assessed, actioned, and resolved in a timely and efficient manner?

442. Were the budget estimates reasonable?

443. Are multiple estimation methods being employed?

444. Does the Business Model Innovation project have

a formal Business Model Innovation project Charter?

445. Are all key components of a Quality Assurance Plan present?

446. Cost tracking and performance analysis – How will cost tracking and performance analysis be accomplished?

447. Designated small business reserve?

448. Escalation criteria met?

449. Was the Business Model Innovation project schedule reviewed by all stakeholders and formally accepted?

450. Is the quality assurance team identified?

451. Are target dates established for each milestone deliverable?

2.21 Activity Cost Estimates: Business Model Innovation

452. Were escalated issues resolved promptly?

453. How do you manage cost?

454. Did the Business Model Innovation project team have the right skills?

455. Where can you get activity reports?

456. Why do you manage cost?

457. How Award?

458. How many activities should you have?

459. Specific - is the objective clear in terms of what, how, when, and where the situation will be changed?

460. What makes a good expected result statement?

461. Scope statement only direct or indirect costs as well?

462. Would you hire them again?

463. Vac -variance at completion, how much over/ under budget do you expect to be?

464. What cost data should be used to estimate costs during the 2-year follow-up period?

465. Were sponsors and decision makers available when needed outside regularly scheduled meetings?

466. How do you change activities?

467. What is the activity inventory?

468. One way to define activities is to consider how organization employees describe jobs to families and friends. You basically want to know, What do you do?

469. Was it performed on time?

470. In which phase of the acquisition process cycle does source qualifications reside?

471. How do you allocate indirect costs to activities?

2.22 Cost Estimating Worksheet: Business Model Innovation

472. Identify the timeframe necessary to monitor progress and collect data to determine how the selected measure has changed?

473. Does the Business Model Innovation project provide innovative ways for stakeholders to overcome obstacles or deliver better outcomes?

474. What costs are to be estimated?

475. Will the Business Model Innovation project collaborate with the local community and leverage resources?

476. Is it feasible to establish a control group arrangement?

477. Can a trend be established from historical performance data on the selected measure and are the criteria for using trend analysis or forecasting methods met?

478. Who is best positioned to know and assist in identifying corresponding factors?

479. Value pocket identification & quantification what are value pockets?

480. How will the results be shared and to whom?

481. What is the estimated labor cost today based upon this information?

482. What can be included?

483. What happens to any remaining funds not used?

484. What is the purpose of estimating?

485. Ask: are others positioned to know, are others credible, and will others cooperate?

486. What additional Business Model Innovation project(s) could be initiated as a result of this Business Model Innovation project?

487. What will others want?

488. Is the Business Model Innovation project responsive to community need?

2.23 Cost Baseline: Business Model Innovation

489. How likely is it to go wrong?

490. Have the resources used by the Business Model Innovation project been reassigned to other units or Business Model Innovation projects?

491. Impact to environment?

492. Has the Business Model Innovation projected annual cost to operate and maintain the product(s) or service(s) been approved and funded?

493. Does it impact schedule, cost, quality?

494. Is there anything unique in this Business Model Innovation projects scope statement that will affect resources?

495. For what purpose ?

496. Does the suggested change request seem to represent a necessary enhancement to the product?

497. What is the consequence?

498. What is the most important thing to do next to make your Business Model Innovation project successful?

499. Is the requested change request a result

of changes in other Business Model Innovation project(s)?

500. Have all the product or service deliverables been accepted by the customer?

501. How long are you willing to wait before you find out were late?

502. Does a process exist for establishing a cost baseline to measure Business Model Innovation project performance?

503. Who will use corresponding metrics ?

504. Is there anything you need from upper management in order to be successful?

505. Are procedures defined by which the cost baseline may be changed?

2.24 Quality Management Plan: Business Model Innovation

506. How are calibration records kept?

507. What is the audience for the data?

508. Does the Business Model Innovation project have a formal Business Model Innovation project Plan?

509. Written by multiple authors and in multiple writing styles?

510. Documented results available?

511. Who is responsible?

512. How do you decide what information needs to be recorded?

513. Is there a Steering Committee in place?

514. Contradictory information between document sections?

515. What type of in-house testing do you conduct?

516. Who do you send data to?

517. Methodology followed?

518. With the five whys method, the team considers why the issue being explored occurred. do others

then take that initial answer and ask why?

519. Are there processes in place to ensure internal consistency between the source code components?

520. How are records kept in the office?

521. How are changes recorded?

522. Are there trends or hot spots?

523. What are the appropriate test methods to be used?

524. Are you meeting the quality standards?

2.25 Quality Metrics: Business Model Innovation

525. Are quality metrics defined?

526. How should customers provide input?

527. What happens if you get an abnormal result?

528. Which are the right metrics to use?

529. Should a modifier be included?

530. Can visual measures help you to filter visualizations of interest?

531. Is there a set of procedures to capture, analyze and act on quality metrics?

532. Do you stratify metrics by product or site?

533. Did the team meet the Business Model Innovation project success criteria documented in the Quality Metrics Matrix?

534. How effective are your security tests?

535. What percentage are outcome-based?

536. If the defect rate during testing is substantially higher than that of the previous release (or a similar product), then ask: Did you plan for and actually improve testing effectiveness?

537. What level of statistical confidence do you use?

538. What is the benchmark?

539. Where is quality now?

540. There are many reasons to shore up quality-related metrics, and what metrics are important?

541. What are your organizations expectations for its quality Business Model Innovation project?

542. What are your organizations next steps?

2.26 Process Improvement Plan: Business Model Innovation

543. If a process improvement framework is being used, which elements will help the problems and goals listed?

544. Has a process guide to collect the data been developed?

545. Are you making progress on the goals?

546. What is the test-cycle concept?

547. What is the return on investment?

548. Have the supporting tools been developed or acquired?

549. What is quality and how will you ensure it?

550. Does your process ensure quality?

551. What personnel are the sponsors for that initiative?

552. Have the frequency of collection and the points in the process where measurements will be made been determined?

553. To elicit goal statements, do you ask a question such as, What do you want to achieve?

554. Have storage and access mechanisms and procedures been determined?

555. What lessons have you learned so far?

556. Everyone agrees on what process improvement is, right?

557. How do you manage quality?

558. What actions are needed to address the problems and achieve the goals?

559. Where do you want to be?

2.27 Responsibility Assignment Matrix: Business Model Innovation

560. Availability – will the group or the person be available within the necessary time interval?

561. Who is the Business Model Innovation project Manager?

562. The staff characteristics – is the group or the person capable to work together as a team?

563. What simple tool can you use to help identify and prioritize Business Model Innovation project risks that is very low tech and high touch?

564. What do people write/say on status/Business Model Innovation project reports?

565. Cwbs elements to be subcontracted, with identification of subcontractors?

566. Are detailed work packages planned as far in advance as practicable?

567. What expertise is not available in your department?

568. What is the justification?

569. Does the contractors system provide unit or lot costs when applicable?

570. Are all elements of indirect expense identified to overhead cost budgets of Business Model Innovation projections?

571. Are authorized changes being incorporated in a timely manner?

572. Are too many reports done in writing instead of verbally?

573. Will too many Communicating responsibilities tangle the Business Model Innovation project in unnecessary communications?

574. What do you need to implement earned value management?

575. How many hours by each staff member/rate?

576. Is it safe to say you can handle more work or that some tasks you are supposed to do arent worth doing?

577. Are control accounts opened and closed based on the start and completion of work contained therein?

578. What do you do when people do not respond?

2.28 Roles and Responsibilities: Business Model Innovation

579. How well did the Business Model Innovation project Team understand the expectations of specific roles and responsibilities?

580. Influence: what areas of organizational decision making are you able to influence when you do not have authority to make the final decision?

581. Was the expectation clearly communicated?

582. Where are you most strong as a supervisor?

583. Authority: what areas/Business Model Innovation projects in your work do you have the authority to decide upon and act on the already stated decisions?

584. Who: who is involved?

585. Do you take the time to clearly define roles and responsibilities on Business Model Innovation project tasks?

586. What areas would you highlight for changes or improvements?

587. Be specific; avoid generalities. Thank you and great work alone are insufficient. What exactly do you appreciate and why?

588. What expectations were met?

589. Key conclusions and recommendations: Are conclusions and recommendations relevant and acceptable?

590. Does your vision/mission support a culture of quality data?

591. Once the responsibilities are defined for the Business Model Innovation project, have the deliverables, roles and responsibilities been clearly communicated to every participant?

592. What are your major roles and responsibilities in the area of performance measurement and assessment?

593. Have you ever been a part of this team?

594. Accountabilities: what are the roles and responsibilities of individual team members?

595. Attainable / achievable: the goal is attainable; can you actually accomplish the goal?

596. To decide whether to use a quality measurement, ask how will you know when it is achieved?

597. What is working well within your organizations performance management system?

2.29 Human Resource Management Plan: Business Model Innovation

598. Have all unresolved risks been documented?

599. Does all Business Model Innovation project documentation reside in a common repository for easy access?

600. Are people being developed to meet the challenges of the future?

601. Are Business Model Innovation project leaders committed to this Business Model Innovation project full time?

602. Was the scope definition used in task sequencing?

603. Are the Business Model Innovation project team members located locally to the users/stakeholders?

604. What commitments have been made?

605. Are trade-offs between accepting the risk and mitigating the risk identified?

606. Has the Business Model Innovation project scope been baselined?

607. How do you determine what key skills and talents are needed to meet the objectives. Is your organization primarily focused on a specific industry?

608. Is the current culture aligned with the vision, mission, and values of the department?

609. Does the detailed work plan match the complexity of tasks with the capabilities of personnel?

610. Is there a requirements change management processes in place?

611. Have process improvement efforts been completed before requirements efforts begin?

612. Has the business need been clearly defined?

613. Are quality inspections and review activities listed in the Business Model Innovation project schedule(s)?

2.30 Communications Management Plan: Business Model Innovation

614. Who will use or be affected by the result of a Business Model Innovation project?

615. Who were proponents/opponents?

616. Will messages be directly related to the release strategy or phases of the Business Model Innovation project?

617. How did the term stakeholder originate?

618. What communications method?

619. What is the stakeholders level of authority?

620. Can you think of other people who might have concerns or interests?

621. How is this initiative related to other portfolios, programs, or Business Model Innovation projects?

622. Are stakeholders internal or external?

623. What is Business Model Innovation project communications management?

624. Which stakeholders can influence others?

625. What to learn?

626. What is the political influence?

627. Are there potential barriers between the team and the stakeholder?

628. Who needs to know and how much?

629. What does the stakeholder need from the team?

630. In your work, how much time is spent on stakeholder identification?

631. What are the interrelationships?

2.31 Risk Management Plan: Business Model Innovation

632. Is the process being followed?

633. Why do you want risk management?

634. Mitigation -how can you avoid the risk?

635. Anticipated volatility of the requirements?

636. Is Business Model Innovation project scope stable?

637. How will the Business Model Innovation project know if your organizations risk response actions were effective?

638. How much risk protection can you afford?

639. How is the audit profession changing?

640. Does the Business Model Innovation project team have experience with the technology to be implemented?

641. Was an original risk assessment/risk management plan completed?

642. Are enough people available?

643. What risks are tracked?

644. What things might go wrong?

645. Is security a central objective?

646. What is the impact to the Business Model Innovation project if the item is not resolved in a timely fashion?

647. User involvement: do you have the right users?

648. Are the reports useful and easy to read?

649. How quickly does this item need to be resolved?

2.32 Risk Register: Business Model Innovation

650. What are the assumptions and current status that support the assessment of the risk?

651. What will be done?

652. What can be done about it?

653. Do you require further engagement?

654. What may happen or not go according to plan?

655. What has changed since the last period?

656. What is the probability and impact of the risk occurring?

657. Why would you develop a risk register?

658. Are your objectives at risk?

659. What are you going to do to limit the Business Model Innovation projects risk exposure due to the identified risks?

660. Does the evidence highlight any areas to advance opportunities or foster good relations. If yes what steps will be taken?

661. What evidence do you have to justify the likelihood score of the risk (audit, incident report,

claim, complaints, inspection, internal review)?

662. Have other controls and solutions been implemented in other services which could be applied as an alternative to additional funding?

663. Amongst the action plans and recommendations that you have to introduce are there some that could stop or delay the overall program?

664. What could prevent you delivering on the strategic program objectives and what is being done to mitigate corresponding issues?

665. Preventative actions - planned actions to reduce the likelihood a risk will occur and/or reduce the seriousness should it occur. What should you do now?

666. Who is accountable?

667. What action, if any, has been taken to respond to the risk?

668. What is a Risk?

2.33 Probability and Impact Assessment: Business Model Innovation

669. How will economic events and trends likely affect the Business Model Innovation project?

670. Do benefits and chances of success outweigh potential damage if success is not attained?

671. Do you have a consistent repeatable process that is actually used?

672. How is the Business Model Innovation project going to be managed?

673. Has the need for the Business Model Innovation project been properly established?

674. Are tool mentors available?

675. Should the risk be taken at all?

676. How do the products attain the specifications?

677. Your customers business requirements have suddenly shifted because of a new regulatory statute, what now?

678. Does the Business Model Innovation project team have experience with the technology to be implemented?

679. Are staff committed for the duration of the Business Model Innovation project?

680. Are formal technical reviews part of this process?

681. To what extent is the chosen technology maturing?

682. What are the preparations required for facing difficulties?

683. How well is the risk understood?

684. What should be the external organizations responsibility vis-à-vis total stake in the Business Model Innovation project?

685. Are testing tools available and suitable?

686. What should be done with non-critical risks?

687. What risks does the employee encounter?

2.34 Probability and Impact Matrix: Business Model Innovation

688. How will the consumption pattern change?

689. What do you expect?

690. Can it be enlarged by drawing people from other areas of your organization?

691. What things are likely to change?

692. Are Business Model Innovation project requirements stable?

693. Is the technology to be built new to your organization?

694. What should be the gestation period for the Business Model Innovation project with this technology?

695. What action do you usually take against risks?

696. Which should be probably done NEXT?

697. Amount of reused software?

698. Prioritized components/features?

699. Mandated specific features?

700. How much is the probability of the risk

occurring?

701. Which risks need to move on to Perform Quantitative Risk Analysis?

702. Have you worked with the customer in the past?

703. What will be the likely political environment during the life of the Business Model Innovation project?

704. Are tools for analysis and design available?

705. What are ways to measure and evaluate risks?

706. What are the channels available for distribution to the customer?

2.35 Risk Data Sheet: Business Model Innovation

707. What do people affected think about the need for, and practicality of preventive measures?

708. If it happens, what are the consequences?

709. How reliable is the data source?

710. What can happen?

711. What will be the consequences if it happens?

712. How can hazards be reduced?

713. Has a sensitivity analysis been carried out?

714. What will be the consequences if the risk happens?

715. What is the environment within which you operate (social trends, economic, community values, broad based participation, national directions etc.)?

716. What can you do?

717. How do you handle product safely?

718. Type of risk identified?

719. What actions can be taken to eliminate or remove risk?

720. What are you here for (Mission)?

721. Are new hazards created?

722. During work activities could hazards exist?

723. Whom do you serve (customers)?

724. Who has a vested interest in how you perform as your organization (our stakeholders)?

725. What if client refuses?

2.36 Procurement Management Plan: Business Model Innovation

726. Have all necessary approvals been obtained?

727. Are non-critical path items updated and agreed upon with the teams?

728. Are software metrics formally captured, analyzed and used as a basis for other Business Model Innovation project estimates?

729. Are any non-compliance issues that exist communicated to your organization?

730. Is the assigned Business Model Innovation project manager a PMP (Certified Business Model Innovation project manager) and experienced?

731. Are the Business Model Innovation project plans updated on a frequent basis?

732. Has a provision been made to reassess Business Model Innovation project risks at various Business Model Innovation project stages?

733. Does the Business Model Innovation project have a Quality Culture?

734. Are tasks tracked by hours?

735. Do all stakeholders know how to access the PM repository and where to find the Business Model

Innovation project documentation?

736. Is there a set of procedures defining the scope, procedures, and deliverables defining quality control?

737. Have adequate resources been provided by management to ensure Business Model Innovation project success?

738. Are estimating assumptions and constraints captured?

739. Was the Business Model Innovation project schedule reviewed by all stakeholders and formally accepted?

2.37 Source Selection Criteria: Business Model Innovation

740. Do proposed hours support content and schedule?

741. Why promote competition?

742. Have team members been adequately trained?

743. How can the methods of publicizing the buy be tailored to yield more effective price competition?

744. What does a sample rating scale look like?

745. How will you decide an evaluators write up is sufficient?

746. How do you facilitate evaluation against published criteria?

747. How are oral presentations documented?

748. How can business terms and conditions be improved to yield more effective price competition?

749. What past performance information should be requested?

750. What does an evaluation address and what does a sample resemble?

751. How much weight should be placed on past

performance information?

752. What are the guidelines regarding award without considerations?

753. What are the most common types of rating systems?

754. What are the steps in performing a cost/tech tradeoff?

755. Are considerations anticipated?

756. Are responses to considerations adequate?

757. Is the offeror pricing what is technically proposed?

758. How and when do you enter into Business Model Innovation project Procurement Management?

759. How do you consolidate reviews and analysis of evaluators?

2.38 Stakeholder Management Plan: Business Model Innovation

760. Who might be involved in developing a charter?

761. Who is responsible for the post implementation review process?

762. Are schedule deliverables actually delivered?

763. What is to be the method of release?

764. Are the Business Model Innovation project plans updated on a frequent basis?

765. How accurate and complete is the information?

766. Are parking lot items captured?

767. Which risks pose the highest threat?

768. Are the appropriate IT resources adequate to meet planned commitments?

769. Is there a formal process for updating the Business Model Innovation project baseline?

770. Are you meeting your customers expectations consistently?

771. Are there standards for code development?

772. Are regulatory inspections considered part of

quality control?

773. Will Business Model Innovation project success require up to date information at a moments notice?

774. Will all relevant stakeholders be included within the review process?

2.39 Change Management Plan: Business Model Innovation

775. What is the worst thing that can happen if you chose not to communicate this information?

776. What relationships will change?

777. What did the people around you say about it?

778. Will all field readiness criteria have been practically met prior to training roll-out?

779. When does it make sense to customize?

780. Has the priority for this Business Model Innovation project been set by the Business Unit Management Team?

781. What method and medium would you use to announce a message?

782. Where will the funds come from?

783. What are the major changes to processes?

784. Who might present the most resistance?

785. What is the most cynical response it can receive?

786. What would be an estimate of the total cost for the activities required to carry out the change initiative?

787. Do the proposed users have access to the appropriate documentation?

788. Identify the risk and assess the significance and likelihood of it occurring and plan the contingency What risks may occur upfront?

789. Do you need new systems?

790. Would you need to tailor a special message for each segment of the audience?

791. Who will fund the training?

792. Why is it important?

793. What new competencies will be required for the roles?

794. What provokes organizational change?

3.0 Executing Process Group: Business Model Innovation

795. What areas does the group agree are the biggest success on the Business Model Innovation project?

796. Would you rate yourself as being risk-averse, risk-neutral, or risk-seeking?

797. How do you enter durations, link tasks, and view critical path information?

798. When will the Business Model Innovation project be done?

799. When is the appropriate time to bring the scorecard to Board meetings?

800. How will you avoid scope creep?

801. Is the schedule for the set products being met?

802. What are the typical Business Model Innovation project management skills?

803. Just how important is your work to the overall success of the Business Model Innovation project?

804. How can software assist in Business Model Innovation project communications?

805. It under budget or over budget?

806. When do you share the scorecard with managers?

807. Do the products created live up to the necessary quality?

808. What are the critical steps involved with strategy mapping?

809. Do the partners have sufficient financial capacity to keep up the benefits produced by the programme?

810. What are deliverables of your Business Model Innovation project?

811. Measurable - are the targets measurable?

812. Who will provide training?

813. What are deliverables of your Business Model Innovation project?

3.1 Team Member Status Report: Business Model Innovation

814. Does the product, good, or service already exist within your organization?

815. What is to be done?

816. Are your organizations Business Model Innovation projects more successful over time?

817. Does every department have to have a Business Model Innovation project Manager on staff?

818. Will the staff do training or is that done by a third party?

819. What specific interest groups do you have in place?

820. Why is it to be done?

821. Are the attitudes of staff regarding Business Model Innovation project work improving?

822. Do you have an Enterprise Business Model Innovation project Management Office (EPMO)?

823. How it is to be done?

824. How can you make it practical?

825. Does your organization have the means (staff,

money, contract, etc.) to produce or to acquire the product, good, or service?

826. How does this product, good, or service meet the needs of the Business Model Innovation project and your organization as a whole?

827. Is there evidence that staff is taking a more professional approach toward management of your organizations Business Model Innovation projects?

828. How will resource planning be done?

829. How much risk is involved?

830. When a teams productivity and success depend on collaboration and the efficient flow of information, what generally fails them?

831. The problem with Reward & Recognition Programs is that the truly deserving people all too often get left out. How can you make it practical?

832. Are the products of your organizations Business Model Innovation projects meeting customers objectives?

3.2 Change Request: Business Model Innovation

833. What is a Change Request Form?

834. Who needs to approve change requests?

835. Who is responsible to authorize changes?

836. Has the change been highlighted and documented in the CSCI?

837. How does your organization control changes before and after software is released to a customer?

838. Will the change use memory to the extent that other functions will be not have sufficient memory to operate effectively?

839. Who is included in the change control team?

840. Who is responsible for the implementation and monitoring of all measures?

841. Are you implementing itil processes?

842. Are change requests logged and managed?

843. Where do changes come from?

844. Are there requirements attributes that are strongly related to the occurrence of defects and failures?

845. Are there requirements attributes that are strongly related to the complexity and size?

846. Screen shots or attachments included in a Change Request?

847. Will all change requests be unconditionally tracked through this process?

848. What are the requirements for urgent changes?

849. What is the relationship between requirements attributes and reliability?

850. How is the change documented (format, content, storage)?

851. What are the basic mechanics of the Change Advisory Board (CAB)?

852. How shall the implementation of changes be recorded?

3.3 Change Log: Business Model Innovation

853. Is the change request within Business Model Innovation project scope?

854. Is the change request open, closed or pending?

855. When was the request submitted?

856. Do the described changes impact on the integrity or security of the system?

857. Should a more thorough impact analysis be conducted?

858. How does this change affect scope?

859. How does this relate to the standards developed for specific business processes?

860. Who initiated the change request?

861. When was the request approved?

862. Is this a mandatory replacement?

863. How does this change affect the timeline of the schedule?

864. Is the requested change request a result of changes in other Business Model Innovation project(s)?

865. Will the Business Model Innovation project fail if the change request is not executed?

866. Is the change backward compatible without limitations?

867. Does the suggested change request represent a desired enhancement to the products functionality?

868. Is the submitted change a new change or a modification of a previously approved change?

3.4 Decision Log: Business Model Innovation

869. It becomes critical to track and periodically revisit both operational effectiveness; Are you noticing all that you need to, and are you interpreting what you see effectively?

870. What alternatives/risks were considered?

871. Linked to original objective?

872. How effective is maintaining the log at facilitating organizational learning?

873. Is everything working as expected?

874. How consolidated and comprehensive a story can you tell by capturing currently available incident data in a central location and through a log of key decisions during an incident?

875. What is the line where eDiscovery ends and document review begins?

876. Is your opponent open to a non-traditional workflow, or will it likely challenge anything you do?

877. What is the average size of your matters in an applicable measurement?

878. Does anything need to be adjusted?

879. How do you know when you are achieving it?

880. What was the rationale for the decision?

881. How does provision of information, both in terms of content and presentation, influence acceptance of alternative strategies?

882. At what point in time does loss become unacceptable?

883. Who is the decisionmaker?

884. Who will be given a copy of this document and where will it be kept?

885. Adversarial environment. is your opponent open to a non-traditional workflow, or will it likely challenge anything you do?

886. Decision-making process; how will the team make decisions?

887. How does an increasing emphasis on cost containment influence the strategies and tactics used?

888. Behaviors; what are guidelines that the team has identified that will assist them with getting the most out of team meetings?

3.5 Quality Audit: Business Model Innovation

889. Does everyone know what they are supposed to be doing, how and why?

890. Is there a written corporate quality policy?

891. Is the process of self review, learning and improvement endemic throughout your organization?

892. Are training programs documented?

893. How does your organization know that the range and quality of its accommodation, catering and transportation services are appropriately effective and constructive?

894. How does your organization know that its support services planning and management systems are appropriately effective and constructive?

895. Is your organizations resource allocation system properly aligned with its collection of intentions?

896. Are storage areas and reconditioning operations designed to prevent mix-ups and assure orderly handling of both the distressed and reconditioned devices?

897. Do prior clients have a positive opinion of your organization?

898. Does the supplier use a formal quality system?

899. How does your organization know that it is appropriately effective and constructive in preparing its staff for organizational aspirations?

900. Is there any content that may be legally actionable?

901. What are the main things that hinder your ability to do a good job?

902. Will the evidence likely be sufficient and appropriate?

903. If your organization thinks it is doing something well, can it prove this?

904. Does the report read coherently?

905. How does your organization know that its planning processes are appropriately effective and constructive?

906. How does your organization know that its staff financial services are appropriately effective and constructive?

907. What is your organizations greatest strength?

3.6 Team Directory: Business Model Innovation

908. How does the team resolve conflicts and ensure tasks are completed?

909. When will you produce deliverables?

910. Who will report Business Model Innovation project status to all stakeholders?

911. What needs to be communicated?

912. When does information need to be distributed?

913. Where will the product be used and/or delivered or built when appropriate?

914. Decisions: what could be done better to improve the quality of the constructed product?

915. Who should receive information (all stakeholders)?

916. Why is the work necessary?

917. Process decisions: do invoice amounts match accepted work in place?

918. Timing: when do the effects of communication take place?

919. Where should the information be distributed?

920. Process decisions: are contractors adequately prosecuting the work?

921. Does a Business Model Innovation project team directory list all resources assigned to the Business Model Innovation project?

922. Who are your stakeholders (customers, sponsors, end users, team members)?

923. Process decisions: which organizational elements and which individuals will be assigned management functions?

924. Who will write the meeting minutes and distribute?

925. Is construction on schedule?

926. What are you going to deliver or accomplish?

3.7 Team Operating Agreement: Business Model Innovation

927. What resources can be provided for the team in terms of equipment, space, time for training, protected time and space for meetings, and travel allowances?

928. Have you established procedures that team members can follow to work effectively together, such as a team operating agreement?

929. Do you prevent individuals from dominating the meeting?

930. Does your team need access to all documents and information at all times?

931. Do you vary your voice pace, tone and pitch to engage participants and gain involvement?

932. Are leadership responsibilities shared among team members (versus a single leader)?

933. Did you delegate tasks such as taking meeting minutes, presenting a topic and soliciting input?

934. Do you brief absent members after they view meeting notes or listen to a recording?

935. What types of accommodations will be formulated and put in place for sustaining the team?

936. Resource allocation: how will individual team members account for time and expenses, and how will this be allocated in the team budget?

937. Do you listen for voice tone and word choice to understand the meaning behind words?

938. What administrative supports will be put in place to support the team and the teams supervisor?

939. How do you want to be thought of and known within your organization?

940. What is a Virtual Team?

941. Do you use a parking lot for any items that are important and outside of the agenda?

942. Have you set the goals and objectives of the team?

943. How will you divide work equitably?

944. Do team members reside in more than two countries?

945. Why does your organization want to participate in teaming?

946. Do you send out the agenda and meeting materials in advance?

3.8 Team Performance Assessment: Business Model Innovation

947. To what degree does the teams purpose constitute a broader, deeper aspiration than just accomplishing short-term goals?

948. Can familiarity breed backup?

949. To what degree are fresh input and perspectives systematically caught and added (for example, through information and analysis, new members, and senior sponsors)?

950. To what degree are staff involved as partners in the improvement process?

951. Which situations call for a more extreme type of adaptiveness in which team members actually re-define roles?

952. To what degree does the teams work approach provide opportunity for members to engage in fact-based problem solving?

953. What are teams?

954. To what degree will the team adopt a concrete, clearly understood, and agreed-upon approach that will result in achievement of the teams goals?

955. To what degree do all members feel responsible for all agreed-upon measures?

956. Individual task proficiency and team process behavior: what is important for team functioning?

957. Is there a particular method of data analysis that you would recommend as a means of demonstrating that method variance is not of great concern for a given dataset?

958. To what degree are the goals realistic?

959. What makes opportunities more or less obvious?

960. What do you think is the most constructive thing that could be done now to resolve considerations and disputes about method variance?

961. To what degree can the team ensure that all members are individually and jointly accountable for the teams purpose, goals, approach, and work-products?

962. What are you doing specifically to develop the leaders around you?

963. How hard did you try to make a good selection?

964. To what degree do members understand and articulate the same purpose without relying on ambiguous abstractions?

965. How does Business Model Innovation project termination impact Business Model Innovation project team members?

966. To what degree are corresponding categories of

skills either actually or potentially represented across the membership?

3.9 Team Member Performance Assessment: Business Model Innovation

967. Which training platform formats (i.e., mobile, virtual, videogame-based) were implemented in your effort(s)?

968. Does adaptive training work?

969. How often should assessments be conducted?

970. How often are assessments to be conducted?

971. Where can team members go for more detailed information on performance measurement and assessment?

972. What is needed for effective data teams?

973. How do you work together to improve teaching and learning?

974. Do the goals support your organizations goals?

975. How was the determination made for which training platforms would be used (i.e., media selection)?

976. How are evaluation results utilized?

977. How is assessment information achieved, stored?

978. To what degree does the teams approach to its work allow for modification and improvement over time?

979. Are any governance changes sufficient to impact achievement?

980. Is there reluctance to join a team?

981. What is the Business Management Oversight Process?

982. How does your team work together?

983. What are the standards or expectations for success?

984. How do you create a self-sustaining capacity for a collaborative culture?

985. How do you determine which data are the most important to use, analyze, or review?

3.10 Issue Log: Business Model Innovation

986. Who have you worked with in past, similar initiatives?

987. How do you manage communications?

988. How do you reply to this question; you am new here and managing this major program. How do you suggest you build your network?

989. What is a Stakeholder?

990. Are there common objectives between the team and the stakeholder?

991. How were past initiatives successful?

992. Which stakeholders are thought leaders, influences, or early adopters?

993. Do you feel a register helps?

994. Are you constantly rushing from meeting to meeting?

995. Is access to the Issue Log controlled?

996. What approaches to you feel are the best ones to use?

997. What approaches do you use?

998. Where do team members get information?

999. Are the Business Model Innovation project issues uniquely identified, including to which product they refer?

1000. Are stakeholder roles recognized by your organization?

4.0 Monitoring and Controlling Process Group: Business Model Innovation

1001. Are the services being delivered?

1002. Key stakeholders to work with. How many potential communications channels exist on the Business Model Innovation project?

1003. Is the verbiage used appropriate and understandable?

1004. How will staff learn how to use the deliverables?

1005. How is agile Business Model Innovation project management done?

1006. What areas were overlooked on this Business Model Innovation project?

1007. What good practices or successful experiences or transferable examples have been identified?

1008. How well did the chosen processes fit the needs of the Business Model Innovation project?

1009. Did the Business Model Innovation project team have enough people to execute the Business Model Innovation project plan?

1010. How well did you do?

1011. What areas does the group agree are the biggest success on the Business Model Innovation project?

1012. Based on your Business Model Innovation project communication management plan, what worked well?

1013. Is there adequate validation on required fields?

1014. How to ensure validity, quality and consistency?

1015. What are the goals of the program?

4.1 Project Performance Report: Business Model Innovation

1016. To what degree do team members articulate the teams work approach?

1017. To what degree do team members frequently explore the teams purpose and its implications?

1018. To what degree are sub-teams possible or necessary?

1019. To what degree are the demands of the task compatible with and converge with the relationships of the informal organization?

1020. To what degree does the teams work approach provide opportunity for members to engage in results-based evaluation?

1021. To what degree does the information network communicate information relevant to the task?

1022. To what degree can team members vigorously define the teams purpose in considerations with others who are not part of the functioning team?

1023. To what degree will the approach capitalize on and enhance the skills of all team members in a manner that takes into consideration other demands on members of the team?

1024. To what degree are the teams goals and

objectives clear, simple, and measurable?

1025. Next Steps?

1026. To what degree will new and supplemental skills be introduced as the need is recognized?

1027. To what degree does the team possess adequate membership to achieve its ends?

1028. To what degree does the formal organization make use of individual resources and meet individual needs?

1029. How will procurement be coordinated with other Business Model Innovation project aspects, such as scheduling and performance reporting?

1030. To what degree does the teams purpose contain themes that are particularly meaningful and memorable?

1031. To what degree is there a sense that only the team can succeed?

1032. To what degree do members articulate the goals beyond the team membership?

1033. To what degree do the structures of the formal organization motivate taskrelevant behavior and facilitate task completion?

1034. To what degree can the cognitive capacity of individuals accommodate the flow of information?

4.2 Variance Analysis: Business Model Innovation

1035. Are material costs reported within the same period as that in which BCWP is earned for that material?

1036. Are the actual costs used for variance analysis reconcilable with data from the accounting system?

1037. Does the contractors system identify work accomplishment against the schedule plan?

1038. Can process improvements lead to unfavorable variances?

1039. Wbs elements contractually specified for reporting of status to your organization (lowest level only)?

1040. Contract line items and end items?

1041. Are all authorized tasks assigned to identified organizational elements?

1042. Is the anticipated (firm and potential) business base Business Model Innovation projected in a rational, consistent manner?

1043. What is the expected future profitability of each customer?

1044. What is the dollar amount of the fluctuation?

1045. Did a new competitor enter the market?

1046. Did your organization lose existing customers and/or gain new customers?

1047. How does the monthly budget compare to the actual experience?

1048. Did an existing competitor change strategy?

1049. Are the wbs and organizational levels for application of the Business Model Innovation projected overhead costs identified?

1050. Are management actions taken to reduce indirect costs when there are significant adverse variances?

4.3 Earned Value Status: Business Model Innovation

1051. Verification is a process of ensuring that the developed system satisfies the stakeholders agreements and specifications; Are you building the product right? What do you verify?

1052. How much is it going to cost by the finish?

1053. What is the unit of forecast value?

1054. When is it going to finish?

1055. If earned value management (EVM) is so good in determining the true status of a Business Model Innovation project and Business Model Innovation project its completion, why is it that hardly any one uses it in information systems related Business Model Innovation projects?

1056. Where are your problem areas?

1057. Earned value can be used in almost any Business Model Innovation project situation and in almost any Business Model Innovation project environment. it may be used on large Business Model Innovation projects, medium sized Business Model Innovation projects, tiny Business Model Innovation projects (in cut-down form), complex and simple Business Model Innovation projects and in any market sector. some people, of course, know all about earned value, they have used it for years - but perhaps not as effectively as they could have?

1058. How does this compare with other Business Model Innovation projects?

1059. Validation is a process of ensuring that the developed system will actually achieve the stakeholders desired outcomes; Are you building the right product? What do you validate?

1060. Where is evidence-based earned value in your organization reported?

1061. Are you hitting your Business Model Innovation projects targets?

4.4 Risk Audit: Business Model Innovation

1062. What can be measured?

1063. Are policies communicated to all affected?

1064. What resources are needed to achieve program results?

1065. Is all expenditure authorised through an identified process?

1066. The halo effect in business risk audits: can strategic risk assessment bias auditor judgment about accounting details?

1067. Does willful intent modify risk-based auditing?

1068. Is the number of people on the Business Model Innovation project team adequate to do the job?

1069. Do you have a mechanism for managing change?

1070. Have risks been considered with an insurance broker or provider and suitable insurance cover been arranged?

1071. Do you have financial policies and procedures in place to guide officers of your organization/treasurer/ general members?

1072. Are procedures developed to respond to foreseeable emergencies and communicated to all involved?

1073. Are duties out-of-class?

1074. Does your auditor understand your business?

1075. Is your organization an exempt employer for payroll tax purposes?

1076. What are the differences and similarities between strategic and operational risks in your organization?

1077. Are all financial transactions accurately recorded (receipted, banked)?

1078. Are risk assessments documented?

1079. Number of users of the product?

1080. How do you prioritize risks?

4.5 Contractor Status Report: Business Model Innovation

1081. What was the actual budget or estimated cost for your organizations services?

1082. Describe how often regular updates are made to the proposed solution. Are corresponding regular updates included in the standard maintenance plan?

1083. What was the overall budget or estimated cost?

1084. Who can list a Business Model Innovation project as organization experience, your organization or a previous employee of your organization?

1085. What was the budget or estimated cost for your organizations services?

1086. What are the minimum and optimal bandwidth requirements for the proposed solution?

1087. If applicable; describe your standard schedule for new software version releases. Are new software version releases included in the standard maintenance plan?

1088. What was the final actual cost?

1089. How does the proposed individual meet each requirement?

1090. Are there contractual transfer concerns?

1091. What process manages the contracts?

1092. What is the average response time for answering a support call?

1093. How long have you been using the services?

1094. How is risk transferred?

4.6 Formal Acceptance: Business Model Innovation

1095. What was done right?

1096. Do you perform formal acceptance or burn-in tests?

1097. Have all comments been addressed?

1098. Did the Business Model Innovation project achieve its MOV?

1099. Do you buy-in installation services?

1100. How does your team plan to obtain formal acceptance on your Business Model Innovation project?

1101. What lessons were learned about your Business Model Innovation project management methodology?

1102. Do you buy pre-configured systems or build your own configuration?

1103. What is the Acceptance Management Process?

1104. What can you do better next time?

1105. Who would use it?

1106. Was the Business Model Innovation project

managed well?

1107. Was the Business Model Innovation project goal achieved?

1108. Does it do what client said it would?

1109. Did the Business Model Innovation project manager and team act in a professional and ethical manner?

1110. What function(s) does it fill or meet?

1111. General estimate of the costs and times to complete the Business Model Innovation project?

1112. Does it do what Business Model Innovation project team said it would?

1113. How well did the team follow the methodology?

1114. Was business value realized?

5.0 Closing Process Group: Business Model Innovation

1115. Were the outcomes different from the already stated planned?

1116. Is this a follow-on to a previous Business Model Innovation project?

1117. Were cost budgets met?

1118. When will the Business Model Innovation project be done?

1119. What was learned?

1120. How will you do it?

1121. Just how important is your work to the overall success of the Business Model Innovation project?

1122. What were things that you did well, and could improve, and how?

1123. Is there a clear cause and effect between the activity and the lesson learned?

1124. How well did the team follow the chosen processes?

1125. Did the Business Model Innovation project team have the right skills?

1126. What areas does the group agree are the biggest success on the Business Model Innovation project?

1127. Who are the Business Model Innovation project stakeholders?

1128. Is this an updated Business Model Innovation project Proposal Document?

1129. Did the Business Model Innovation project management methodology work?

1130. Did the delivered product meet the specified requirements and goals of the Business Model Innovation project?

1131. What areas were overlooked on this Business Model Innovation project?

5.1 Procurement Audit: Business Model Innovation

1132. Where an electronic auction was used to bid, were all required specifications given equally to tenderers?

1133. Is there no evidence of unauthorized release of information or seemingly unnecessary contacts with bidders personnel during the evaluation and negotiation processes?

1134. When competitive dialogue was used, did the contracting authority provide sufficient justification for the use of this procedure and was the contract actually particularly complex?

1135. Is there no evidence of collusion between bidders?

1136. Are controls proportionated to risks?

1137. Are fixed asset values recorded at historical cost?

1138. Does the individual having check-signing responsibility review the use of the signature plates?

1139. Are unusual uses of organization funds investigated?

1140. Were the specifications of the contract determined free from influence of particular interests of consultants, experts or other economic operators?

1141. Are staff members evaluated in accordance with the terms of existing negotiated agreements?

1142. Are individuals with check-signing responsibility prohibited from signing blank checks?

1143. Were any additional works or deliveries admissible, without recourse to a new procurement procedure?

1144. Does your organization have a purchasing policy ?

1145. Were bids properly evaluated?

1146. Is procurement execution duly monitored and documented?

1147. Does the contract meet criteria of completeness and consistency?

1148. Are incentives to deliver on time and in quantity properly specified?

1149. Are existing suppliers that have a special right to be consulted being contacted?

1150. Do you learn from benchmarking your own practices with international standards?

1151. Is the routing of copies of purchase order forms defined?

5.2 Contract Close-Out: Business Model Innovation

1152. Change in knowledge?

1153. Change in circumstances?

1154. Was the contract sufficiently clear so as not to result in numerous disputes and misunderstandings?

1155. Have all contracts been completed?

1156. Was the contract type appropriate?

1157. What is capture management?

1158. How is the contracting office notified of the automatic contract close-out?

1159. Have all contract records been included in the Business Model Innovation project archives?

1160. What happens to the recipient of services?

1161. Have all acceptance criteria been met prior to final payment to contractors?

1162. Are the signers the authorized officials?

1163. Have all contracts been closed?

1164. Parties: who is involved?

1165. Has each contract been audited to verify acceptance and delivery?

1166. Why Outsource?

1167. How/when used ?

1168. Parties: Authorized?

1169. Was the contract complete without requiring numerous changes and revisions?

1170. Change in attitude or behavior?

1171. How does it work?

5.3 Project or Phase Close-Out: Business Model Innovation

1172. What information is each stakeholder group interested in?

1173. Who is responsible for award close-out?

1174. What stakeholder group needs, expectations, and interests are being met by the Business Model Innovation project?

1175. Planned completion date?

1176. Who exerted influence that has positively affected or negatively impacted the Business Model Innovation project?

1177. Who controlled key decisions that were made?

1178. Were risks identified and mitigated?

1179. Is the lesson based on actual Business Model Innovation project experience rather than on independent research?

1180. In preparing the Lessons Learned report, should it reflect a consensus viewpoint, or should the report reflect the different individual viewpoints?

1181. Is the lesson significant, valid, and applicable?

1182. Was the schedule met?

1183. What is this stakeholder expecting?

1184. What process was planned for managing issues/ risks?

1185. Can the lesson learned be replicated?

1186. What are the marketing communication needs for each stakeholder?

1187. How much influence did the stakeholder have over others?

1188. What were the desired outcomes?

5.4 Lessons Learned: Business Model Innovation

1189. Was the purpose of the Business Model Innovation project, the end products and success criteria clearly defined and agreed at the start?

1190. How mature are the observations?

1191. What mistakes did you successfully avoid making?

1192. Where could you improve?

1193. Was any formal risk assessment carried out at the start of the Business Model Innovation project, and was this followed up during the Business Model Innovation project?

1194. What would you approach differently next time?

1195. How effective were the techniques used to prepare you and your organization for the impact of the changes brought about by the product or service produced by the Business Model Innovation project?

1196. How closely did deliverables match what was defined within the Business Model Innovation project Scope?

1197. What were the success factors?

1198. How timely was the training you received in

preparation for the use of the product/service?

1199. What are the influence patterns?

1200. What could have been improved?

1201. What were the major enablers to a quick response?

1202. Where do you go from here?

1203. What regulatory constraints impact the case?

1204. Who managed most of the communication within the Business Model Innovation project?

1205. Do you have any real problems?

1206. How much time is required for the task?

1207. Do you conduct the engineering tests?

1208. What were the problems encountered in the Business Model Innovation project-functional area relationship, why, and how could they be fixed?

Index

269

process 1-6, 8, 12, 32-33, 37-38, 40, 42-43, 54, 60-62, 64-66, 68-75, 77, 86, 96-102, 104, 131-132, 138, 142, 144-146, 148, 150-153, 156, 169, 173-174, 177, 182, 186, 191-192, 198, 201, 205-206, 215-216, 219, 224, 228-229, 231-232, 235-236, 239, 242, 246, 248-250, 253-254, 256, 263

processes 50, 62-68, 72, 75, 101-102, 131-132, 158, 188, 198, 217, 223, 225, 230, 242, 256, 258

produce 71, 131, 170, 222, 231

produced 64, 89, 220, 264

producing 148

product 1, 12, 56, 74, 118, 139, 150, 165, 177, 185-186, 189, 209, 221-222, 231, 241, 248-249, 251, 257, 264-265

production 32, 88, 112

products 1, 26-27, 56, 108, 116, 138, 149, 179, 205, 219-220, 222, 226, 264

profession 201

program 19, 58, 61, 104, 204, 240, 243, 250

programme 220

programs 199, 222, 229

progress 38, 58, 84, 109, 125, 133, 138, 150, 183, 191

prohibited 158, 259

project 2-4, 6-8, 10, 19, 23-24, 27, 37, 48, 64, 68, 74, 78, 94, 97, 101-102, 111-112, 116-117, 119, 124, 129-145, 147-148, 150-155, 159-163, 165-168, 171-181, 183-187, 189-190, 193-199, 201-202, 205-208, 211-212, 214-217, 219-222, 225-226, 231-232, 236, 241-245, 248, 250, 252, 254-257, 260, 262, 264-265

projected 185, 246-247

projects 2, 53, 114, 120, 130, 133, 148, 151, 154, 159, 174, 177, 185, 195, 199, 203, 221-222, 248-249

promote 56, 213

promptly 181

proofing 86

proper 104

properly 12, 35, 40, 131, 156, 205, 229, 259

proponents 199

proposal 145, 165-166, 257

proposals 103

proposed 22, 48, 54, 80, 89, 141, 147, 213-214, 218, 252

protect 61, 115, 140

protected 71, 233

protection 126, 201

provide 19, 68, 109, 117, 123, 135, 137, 175, 178, 183, 189, 193, 220, 235, 244, 258

CPSIA information can be obtained
at www.ICGtesting.com
Printed in the USA
BVHW041757290719
554530BV00036B/932/P

9 780655 826699